THE
MURDER GAME

by
CONSTANCE COX

SAMUEL   FRENCH

LONDON
NEW YORK   TORONTO   SYDNEY   HOLLYWOOD

THE MURDER GAME

First produced at the Connaught Theatre, Worthing, on March 31st, 1976, with the following cast of characters:

Brian Hamilton	John Bentley
Sheila Hamilton, his wife	Carol Snape
Gerry Stephens	Mark Lester
June Maitland	Shelley Borkum

The play directed by Nicolas Young
Set design by Vivienne Corringham

ACT I   An evening in February

ACT II
   Scene 1   Morning, six months later
   Scene 2   Evening, two weeks later
   Scene 3   Evening, three weeks later

The action of the play passes in the living-room of Brian Hamilton's house near Dorking, in the stockbroker belt

Time – the present

ACT I*

A sitting-room in the stockbroker belt near Dorking. A February evening

The room is furnished in a modern manner with a small bar at one end of the room. The front door leads straight into the room from a porch in which stand pot plants. It is important that anyone entering the front door should be immediately visible to the audience. There is a window in one wall, and a door to the kitchen. A wrought iron staircase leads from the room at the back. The room has an air of prosperity

When the Curtain rises, the room is in darkness. After a moment a car is heard approaching. As it nears the house there is suddenly a scream of brakes, and the sound of a skid. The engine roars, then it is switched off. A car door bangs. Brian Hamilton is heard speaking off

Brian (*off*) Are you all right?
Gerry (*off*) I'm not sure—I think so.
Brian (*off*) Wait till I get the door open.

There is the sound of a key in the lock, and the front door is opened. Brian Hamilton switches on the lights. He is a man of about forty, handsome in a florid way. There is a suggestion of a sporting background about him. He turns at the door

Brian Come on in. Let's have a look at you.

Gerry Stephens enters. He is about twenty-two, but looks much younger. He is dressed in jeans and anorak. His hair is well-groomed, and he is quite beautiful

Gerry I've got a bag out there somewhere.
Brian Wait a minute. I'll find it.

Brian switches on a porch light and goes out

Gerry feels his left arm and rubs it

Brian returns with a hold-all

Brian This it?
Gerry Yes. Thank you.

Brian switches off the porch light and turns to see Gerry rubbing his arm

---

*N.B. Paragraph 3 on page ii of this Acting Edition regarding photocopying and video-recording should be carefully read.

Brian Are you hurt? I didn't think I touched you.

Gerry You didn't. It was a tree. As I jumped out of the way I fell against it.

Brian God, it was a near thing, though! I could do with a drink. How about you?

Gerry No, thank you. I don't drink.

Brian Oh, come on, you must have something. You must be pretty shaken up. I know I am.

Gerry I'll have a Coke, then, if you've got one.

Brian Coke? (*He goes to the bar*) I think we have. Yes. Like some rum in it?

Gerry No, just as it is, thanks. Don't trouble about a glass. I'll drink it from the can.

Brian Just as you like. (*He brings the can to him, then returns to bar to pour himself a whisky*)

Gerry You're being awfully decent about this. After all, it was my fault. (*He sits*)

Brian Yes, it damn well was. Though the motorist is always blamed if he hits someone—never the pedestrian. What the devil were you doing walking in the middle of our drive? I don't know you, do I?

Gerry No.

Brian Were you coming to see Sheila?

Gerry Who?

Brian My wife. Mrs Hamilton.

Gerry No.

Brian Well, what then? Did you mistake the place?

Gerry No, I was looking for somewhere to sleep.

Brian Sleep?

Gerry Yes.

Brian You mean you thought the house was empty and you were going to break in?

Gerry Oh, no, I was making for that little gazebo place at the end of your garden. I was going to bunk down there.

Brian Well, you're cool, I must say.

Gerry I wouldn't have done any harm. I'd have been gone before you were about in the morning.

Brian I'm out of my depth. You don't look like a tramp or a hippie . . .

Gerry I'm not.

Brian What are you, then? One of these odd-bods who just wander about all over the place—being a general bloody nuisance?

Gerry I do get about. But I prefer to be on my own. You never know who you may meet.

Brian I can imagine.

Gerry Not everyone's as decent as you are, though. I wonder you didn't kick me all the way down your drive.

Brian I won't say I didn't feel like it. Where are you making for?

Gerry (*smiling and shrugging*) Just anywhere.

Brian Don't you have a home and parents?

Gerry Oh, yes. I send them a postcard every now and then.
Brian That's nice of you. When did you cut loose?
Gerry About four years ago when my mother married again.
Brian Didn't you get on with your step-father?
Gerry No. Nobody could. He's a bastard. I'm not as young as I look,
you know. I'm twenty-two.
Brian As much as that! I took you for about sixteen.
Gerry Yes, everybody does. It's very useful.
Brian How do you mean?
Gerry Well, people are much more sympathetic if they think you're only
a kid. (*Smiling*) I shouldn't have told you, should I?
Brian It doesn't matter. I wasn't intending to give you anything. But surely
you don't mean to go on like this for the rest of your life?
Gerry Oh, no. One of these days I expect I shall find someone I like and
settle down with them.
Brian What about money?
Gerry Oh, I make plenty. There are ways, you know.

The telephone rings. Brian answers it

Brian Brian Hamilton. . . . Oh, Sheila! . . . What, at this time of night?
. . . Oh, I didn't realize you were so near; though what the devil there is
to talk about—the whole thing's settled. . . . Oh, all right. I'll expect
you in about ten minutes. (*He hangs up*)
Gerry Would you like me to go now?
Brian There's no immediate hurry. (*He drains his glass*)
Gerry But you've got someone coming.
Brian I'm getting myself something to eat first. Are you hungry?
Gerry Well—if you've got a sandwich.
Brian I'll see what there is.

Brian goes into the kitchen

*Gerry replaces his Coke can on the bar and wanders round the room. He stops
at the record player, looks at the disc on it, and starts the player. After a few
moments, music sounds softly. Then Gerry sees a recess which contains a
number of silver trophies. He takes one down and looks at it; replaces it and
moves to an occasional table on which is an engraved cigarette box. He picks
it up and reads the inscription on it, then puts the box down again*

Brian enters, carrying a tray on which are plates and bread and cheese

Brian (*jerking his head towards the record player*) Do you mind switching
that off.
Gerry Sorry. I thought it was rather a nice tune.
Brian (*setting down the tray*) I happen to loathe it.

Gerry stops the player

Brian There's only bread and cheese. We'll have to make do with that.

They sit and eat

Gerry Suits me fine. You've got a lot of trophies. Are you still a racing driver?

Brian Good Lord no! I gave it up about ten years ago.

Gerry Why? You must have been good.

Brian I was. I still am. If I weren't, right now you'd be a bloody mess spread all over the drive. But racing's different. It's split-second timing—tremendous concentration—thinking ahead all the time, and other attributes as well.

Gerry (*smiling*) Nerves of steel, as they say.

Brian Yes, that just about describes it. When you're past your peak you still think your driving's as good as ever, but the stop-watch proves you wrong. And when you begin to think of danger—that's when you know you're finished.

Gerry But it was good while it lasted?

Brian It was great. The shouting crowds—the girls going mad over you—the laurel wreaths and the champagne. Even now I get something of the old excitement when I take out a really super hot-rod job to test, and a few kids gather round.

Gerry Is that what you do now—test cars?

Brian I'm a motoring correspondent. Those articles you read—well, *you* wouldn't—but those articles in the motoring columns of newspapers and the auto magazines, are mostly written by chaps with my sort of background. Some of us, if we've saved enough, open garages or do specialist tuning, but I didn't come out with that sort of money.

Gerry (*looking round*) Still—so long as one of you has it.

Brian (*going to the bar*) You're a sharp-sighted little bastard, aren't you?

Gerry I know a stockbroker belt when I see one. Was she one of the adoring crowd?

Brian Yes. She was also Harvey's components. That wouldn't mean anything to you, but her father made gearboxes. Damn good ones. His wedding present to her was a quarter of a million.

Gerry (*holding up his bread and cheese*) You could hardly expect her to be able to cook as well.

Brian (*shortly*) That's another story. (*Holding up a Coke can*) Do you want any more of this gut-rot?

Gerry No, thanks. I'll be on my way. Am I allowed to use the summer house or will she object?

Brian She won't know anything about it. She's not staying. Do you want a blanket or anything?

Gerry No, I've got a sleeping-bag in here. (*He moves to the porch door*)

A car is heard coming up the drive

Gerry That was quick. She must drive as fast as you do.

Brian You'd better go out the back way. Through there (*He indicates the kitchen*)

Gerry Will do. (*He picks up the hold-all*) Well, thanks for the hospitality. My name's Gerry Stephens, by the way.

Brian Mine's Brian Hamilton. (*He stacks the plates on the tray*)

Gerry Yes, I saw it.

Brian Of course. Let me know if ever you want to buy a second-hand car. I'll see they don't rook you. Good luck.

Gerry Thanks, and to you. (*He picks up the tray*) I'll take these things into the kitchen as I go, shall I, or she might get the wrong impression.

Gerry exits to the kitchen

The car draws up outside, and the car door bangs. Brian takes the Coke can from the bar and drops it into a waste-bin. He pours himself another drink

Sheila Hamilton enters by the front door. She is an attractive woman of about thirty-five. She wears a trouser suit, and over it a pastel mink coat. She is a blonde

Brian Well, well, well, dead on time, if not before it.

Sheila (*putting her key into her handbag*) You should be used to my punctuality by now. After all, it was your downfall.

Brian Oh, Christ, are we on about that again?

Sheila Is she here?

Brian June? No, of course she isn't.

Sheila I don't know why you say *of course*. She's been here often enough without my knowledge.

Brian Well, she's not here now, and I don't know why you should think so.

Sheila Well, you've left whatever car it is you're testing outside in the drive. You're usually so punctilious about putting these brand-new jobs straight into the garage.

Brian I forgot, that's all.

Sheila And you sounded a bit upset on the telephone just now when I said I wanted to come round.

Brian I'd just had a narrow squeak with the car. Some damn fool jumped out in front of me.

Sheila You didn't hit him?

Brian No, but it was a narrow shave. Do you want a drink?

Sheila Just a small one.

Brian goes to the bar. Sheila sits

Sheila How are you managing, Brian?

Brian All right.

Sheila This room looks a bit of a mess.

Brian Mrs Abbott's been off for a couple of days with 'flu. (*He gives Sheila her drink*) How's that? (*He carries his own*)

Sheila Fine, thanks.

Brian Well—cheers.

Sheila Cheers.

They both drink then fall into an uneasy silence

Brian Where are you staying?

Sheila At the flat in town. I've been away for a few days, though. I was on my way back when I decided to call you.

Brian (*looking at his watch*) You're going to be very late getting back.

Sheila It doesn't matter. There's nobody to mind what time I get in.

Brian I daresay there soon will be.

Sheila Is that supposed to mean something?

Brian Well, you're a pretty attractive proposition. Wealthy young—well, young*ish* divorcee—every mod-con . . .

Sheila We aren't divorced.

Brian It's only a matter of time. Now you've set the wheels in motion . . .

Sheila I haven't.

Brian You haven't?

Sheila No.

Brian But you said two weeks ago when you left here . . .

Sheila I decided to wait.

Brian What for?

Sheila (*bitterly*) You couldn't guess, I suppose? No, that would be too much to ask.

Brian What the bloody hell are you talking about? You storm out of here saying you're getting a divorce. Now you tell me you've done nothing about it and you ask me to guess why.

Sheila I could have changed my mind.

Brian (*alarmed*) Sheila!

Sheila That's not exactly a cry of joy, is it? Don't be afraid. I haven't. Not now, anyway.

Brian Then why the hell did you wait?

Sheila For a damn silly sentimental reason. I just thought you might phone and say you were sorry and wanted to patch things up—something like that. When you didn't . . .

Brian I didn't think there was any hope—after what you said.

Sheila I was in a temper. Hardly surprising when I found my own home was being used as a love nest. And when that bitch turned round and told me how long it had been going on . . .

Brian It wasn't as long as that. She was just angry.

Sheila *She* was angry! I should have apologized, I suppose, and gone meekly away and rung up to find out when the coast was clear!

Brian Anyway, that was the only time I ever brought her here. You *did* say you were going to be away.

Sheila I know. I'm to blame. But for that we might have gone on living happily together—well, living together, at any rate.

Brian And you always said you didn't mind the women who ran after me.

Sheila Ran after you! Oh Brian, you're infantile! Grow up! You haven't had any fans for ten years! Nobody even knows your name any more.

You're grateful if a bunch of kids gather round your Lotus or Jensen or whatever it is you're testing, and ask a couple of damn-fool questions! As far as any fame is concerned, you're a has-been!

Brian (*hotly*) There *are* people who still remember . . .

Sheila I know, I know, the good old Bentley boys of sixty-plus down at the local! The chaps who still say prang and wizard as they down their gins and tonic through their handle-bar moustaches, and are even more out-of-date than you are! I suppose you fell for this girl because she looked at one of your trophies and said, "Darling, you must be marvellous". I hope to God she never finds out just how marvellous darling is!

Brian Look, if you came here just to make another row . . .

Sheila I didn't. I don't know why I'm talking like this. Only I can see now where I went wrong.

Brian How do you mean?

Sheila When we were married. I ought to have let you build another career for yourself, instead of handing you everything on a plate. You could have gone into father's works and earned a proper living. You might even have taken over from him, so that when he died the business didn't have to be sold.

Brian I did suggest it. You know I did.

Sheila Not with any great enthusiasm. Anyway, like a fool, I wanted to have you with me. It wasn't as if there were any problems about money.

Brian No.

They are both silent for a moment

Sheila (*holding out her glass*) Give me another drink.

Brian takes her glass to the bar

You'd better have another yourself as well.

Brian Why?

Sheila Because you're not going to like what I'm going to say next, any more than I shall like saying it. I came here tonight to tell you how you're going to stand in the future—financially, I mean.

Brian That's all arranged! We talked it over before you went.

Sheila I said a few things on the spur of the moment. (*She holds out her hand*) Give me that, please.

Brian hands her the drink

Thank you. You'd hurt me badly, but I was still in love with you. I couldn't forget we'd had eight pretty decent years together—that's why I said I'd be generous. Behind it all, I suppose, I felt sure you wouldn't let me go—that you were bound to get in touch. When you didn't—I began to look at things differently.

Brian You mean you're going back on what you said?

Sheila I mean I no longer see why your marriage to June should be subsidized by my money. I've decided you're old enough to stand on your own feet. (*She listens suddenly*) What was that?

Brian What was what?

Sheila I thought I heard something. Have you been lying to me? Is June upstairs?

Brian No, I swear she isn't! Sheila——

Sheila rises

Sheila I don't believe you. I heard something.

Sheila runs quickly upstairs

Brian looks after her for a moment, then goes to the bar and adds more whisky to his glass

Sheila returns and comes downstairs

Brian Well, did you find her?

Sheila No. I'm sorry. A window catch had come loose and was banging.

Brian I'll have it seen to.

Sheila Don't bother. I'll arrange it when I come back.

Brian (*startled*) Come back?

Sheila Yes. I'm sorry, Brian. I know this is different from what I said before—but I want this house.

Brian But you agreed I should have it! Sheila, you know you did!

Sheila I told you—that was my first generous impulse. Later, looking back on how you'd behaved, I saw no reason why you should.

Brian (*bitterly*) How soon do you want me to clear out?

Sheila There's no hurry. You can stay till the divorce comes through.

Brian Thanks.

Sheila If you think you can afford to.

Brian Are you cutting off the allowance as well?

Sheila My God, you sound surprised!

Brian Of course I am! We talked about all this, and you said it would make no difference to what you'd always given me!

Sheila And if you had any guts you'd have refused to keep it! But no, you wanted everything and June as well, and, like a fool, I thought I'd be noble! Well, now I don't feel noble any more. I just feel hurt, and chucked aside and useless—not even worth the price of a telephone call to say you were sorry.

Brian Would that have made so much difference?

Sheila You didn't phone, so the point doesn't arise. (*She rises and places her glass on the bar*) You won't starve without the allowance. You've got your work.

Brian Thanks very much!

Sheila You earn at least four or five thousand a year. You can live on that.

Brian That's a great prospect, when we've lived at treble that rate for the last eight years.

Sheila I know.

Brian (*rounding on her*) You taught me to live like that!

Sheila But I didn't know you were going to end it, did I?

Brian You've just about bust everything wide open!

Sheila I've done the best thing I can for you, Brian. I was to blame at the beginning—I've admitted that. I gave you the soft life and I spoilt you. When you were racing you were hard and tough and luxury didn't mean much to you. Now you drink too much, you live on your past glories and you work when you feel like it. This way you'll have to face up to life again. And if this girl's any good, she'll help you.

Brian Why don't you say it?

Sheila What?

Brian It hurts you more than it does me.

Sheila I don't like doing it—I haven't liked telling you. I suppose women are more sentimental than men about these things.

Brian You're about as sentimental as an old boot.

Sheila Thank you. (*She picks up her handbag*)

Brian Now you'll set about getting the divorce, I suppose?

Sheila Yes, I'm going to see the solicitor on Monday. He'll be in touch with you. It'll be quite a change, going out and about again, instead of sitting at home, hoping the phone will ring. (*She moves to front door*) Sorry I kept you up so late.

Brian Sheila—wait a minute . . .

Sheila Well?

Brian We could try again, you know.

Sheila You've lost your chance.

Brian No, seriously. If I gave you my word not to see June again . . .

Sheila Stop it!

Brian We could see how it worked out. Just for a few weeks, if you like.

Sheila I don't like.

Brian I would have phoned you if I'd known there was a chance.

Sheila Shut up!

Brian It's not as though June means all that to me. It's always been you.

Sheila Stop it, Brian! You make me ashamed of ever having been in love with you!

Brian What have I said?

Sheila What have you said? You're unbelievable! You can't even see you're telling me plainly that money and comfort were the only things you married me for!

Brian That's not true! You aren't seeing this thing straight!

Sheila I'm seeing things straight for the first time! To think that for nearly eight years I believed you were in love with me! Did you ever love me— or was it a sham right from the beginning? Have you ever loved anybody but yourself?

Brian (*sullenly*) You know I was in love with you.

Sheila No, I don't know it. I know you said the right things—made the right gestures. And because you were the great big hero and it was fun to be chosen from all the rest, I let myself be fooled.

Brian You might let me get a word in edgeways.

Sheila (*quietly*) I don't want to listen to any more from you. You've shown me what you are, and I wouldn't come back to you for all the tea in China. (*She opens the front door*) There are still some clothes of mine here. I'll phone you when I want to collect them, so we can arrange not to meet. And incidentally, when I see the solicitor I shall be changing my will—in case that hadn't occurred to you. (*As she goes through the doorway she looks back*) Don't forget you've left this car outside. Goodbye.

Sheila goes out

Brian stands for a moment, then tosses his drink down and throws the glass violently into a corner

Brian Bloody hell!

Sheila's car is heard to start and drive off

Brian feels in his pocket, takes out his car keys, and exits through the front door, closing it behind him

For a moment the room is empty

Gerry enters from the kitchen. He goes to the bar and gets himself a Coke

The roar of a high-powered car starting is heard. It is driven a little way, then stops. Doors are banged. Gerry moves to the record-player and switches it on. After a moment the music begins

Brian returns—he stares at Gerry

Gerry (*holding up the Coke can*) You didn't mind my helping myself? In the circumstances, I'll pay for it.
Brian What have you come back for? Did you forget something?
Gerry No.
Brian Then do you mind clearing out? I want to go to bed.
Gerry I thought we might have a little chat.
Brian I'm not in the mood for little chats.
Gerry It depends what we talk about, doesn't it?
Brian (*becoming aware of the music*) I told you not to put this damn thing on! (*He switches off the player*) Look, I don't want to be rude, but I've had one hell of a day . . .
Gerry I know. And this evening wasn't so good, either, was it?
Brian How the heck . . . ? Have you been listening?
Gerry Most of the time.
Brian You snooping little bastard! Was it you Sheila heard upstairs?
Gerry Yes. I just had time to nip down the back stairs to the kitchen again. Otherwise she'd have got some new ideas about you, wouldn't she?
Brian That's enough! Get out!
Gerry I haven't finished my Coke.

Brian Damn your bloody Coke! Are you getting out or do I have to kick you out? I've got troubles enough without you.

Gerry I know you have. And here am I, ready to suggest a way to help you out of them, and you won't even listen.

Brian What the hell do you mean? How can *you* help me?

Gerry You'd better shut that door if we're going to talk.

Brian We aren't. You're going.

Gerry All right. If that's how you feel. (*Picking up the hold-all*) It's a pity. It's a nice house and I gather it was a very nice allowance she gave you. Still, if you're perfectly happy to give it all up . . . Oh—(*he feels in his pocket, then goes to the bar and lays a coin on it*)—that's for the Coke. Ten p. (*He walks to the door*) So long.

Brian (*closing the door*) Hold on a bit. If you've really got some idea, I suppose I ought to listen. Though I can't see why you should want to help me.

Gerry You were decent to me, and I'd like to do you a good turn in exchange. (*He sits*) You don't mind if I make myself comfortable? How about having the fire on? It's getting a bit chilly.

Brian (*turning on the fire*) Any more orders?

Gerry Yes, you'd better sit down, too. This is going to be a long session.

Brian Will you damn well come to the point! How can you help me?

Gerry motions him to sit. Reluctantly Brian does so

Gerry First of all, I'm going to ask you a lot of questions. I shall need the right answers.

Brian I'll tell you anything within reason.

Gerry More than that.

Brian All right. More if it's necessary.

Gerry To begin with, I take it this other girl you want to marry hasn't any money.

Brian starts to expostulate

You said you'd answer.

Brian If she had there wouldn't be any problems.

Gerry I just wanted to get the record straight. Have you told anybody Sheila wants a divorce?

Brian Of course not.

Gerry Not even this other girl—what's her name? June.

Brian No. She wants me to marry her, of course, but she doesn't know Sheila and I had this set-to. She's been out of the country, anyway.

Gerry Doing what?

Brian Filming. She does bit parts. She's not well-known or anything.

Gerry Good. Now Sheila. Is she likely to have told anyone?

Brian I don't imagine so. It seems she was expecting me to attempt a reconciliation.

Gerry So—from the point of view of all the people you know, there was no question of a break-up?

Brian None at all.

The Murder Game

Gerry That's fine. Now she said something before she left about altering her will. How does it stand now?
Brian She was leaving me everything.
Gerry That means this house—her money—any other property.
Brian Yes.
Gerry (*thoughtfully*) And she's going to her solicitor next week. Today's Wednesday. That means we've got three days.
Brian For what?
Gerry To stop her changing it.
Brian Her will, you mean?
Gerry Yes.
Brian There's no way of stopping her.
Gerry You're wrong, you know. There is one sure and certain way.
Brian What?
Gerry If she died before next Monday.
Brian (*after a long moment*) Are you suggesting I murder her?
Gerry No.
Brian Then what *are* you suggesting?
Gerry That I murder her.
Brian You!
Gerry I said I'd help you, remember?
Brian But—murder! You're not serious.
Gerry I'm perfectly serious.
Brian But—why should you? You never saw her before tonight!
Gerry What difference does that make?
Brian All the difference in the world! Why should you want to murder my wife? You're not even a friend of hers!
Gerry You must have some funny friends.
Brian Cut out the comic business, will you? Why should you want to murder her?
Gerry Just for the sake of doing it.
Brian You're crazy!
Gerry Oh, no. People do, you know.

Brian moves swiftly to the desk and takes out a service revolver

Brian Get moving! Make it snappy! I'm not very happy at being in here with a homicidal maniac.
Gerry I bet you haven't got a licence for that.
Brian Don't make jokes. Just go.
Gerry You're being very foolish. (*He rises*) If you're nervous about the consequences, I can assure you nobody would know you had a thing to do with it.
Brian Get out!
Gerry The trouble is, I can't even leave an address in case you change your mind.
Brian I shan't change my mind.
Gerry You will, you know, when you have to leave this house and start living on your earnings. Only one bottle of whisky a week instead of

three—no nice new suits in the wardrobe. And one endorsement on your driving licence, and even your job might be in danger. Then you'll wish you'd listened to me. (*He sees the weakening on Brian's face*) Just let me tell you. You don't have to say yes if you don't want to.

Brian I can't stop you talking, I suppose. But in any case, you'd never get away with it.

Gerry Oh, but I should. I have before.

Brian You've killed someone before?

Gerry Only by accident. When I was sixteen.

Brian How?

Gerry In my father's car. I wasn't old enough to have a licence, but I borrowed it one night. I was doing about ninety when some bloody girl ran out into the road in front of me. She just went straight over the bonnet.

Brian What did they do to you?

Gerry Nothing. I was never caught.

Brian Didn't you stop?

Gerry What would have been the point? I guessed she was dead by the way I hit her. It was a very clean kill. No blood or hair on the front of the car; only the bumper stove in a bit. There were no witnesses. Nobody knew what kind of car it was, so it never went any further.

Brian (*sitting; laying the revolver on his knee*) And I suppose what you were going to suggest to me was a similar accident to my wife?

Gerry Oh, no, I don't believe one can get away with that sort of thing twice. Besides, as I said, it wasn't intentional. No, what I've always wanted to do is the really perfect murder.

Brian There's no such thing.

Gerry Oh, yes, there is. Want me to tell you how it could be done?

Brian No. I'm not mixing myself up in anything like that.

Gerry I'm not asking you to.

Brian I'd be mixed up in it even if I had nothing to do with it. I've everything to gain from her death. I should be the prime suspect.

Gerry (*shaking his head*) To be a suspect, you must have a motive.

Brian But I have a motive. I've told you . . .

Gerry No, you haven't. Listen. To all intents and purposes you're a happily married couple. Nobody knows of your intention to break up. Your wife is killed when you're miles away from the spot. There'd be nothing to connect you with it.

Brian But if the police picked you up, they might easily prove I was an accessory before the fact.

Gerry They won't pick me up.

Brian So you say.

Gerry All right. Even if they did—which they won't—they'd have nothing on me. There'll be no fingerprints—nothing missing—no rape—no robbery. I don't even know Sheila Hamilton. What possible motive could I have for killing her?

Brian You could be what you are—a nut case.

Gerry (*smiling*) I don't know why you think it's so difficult to get away

with murder. Don't you know there are hundreds of killings **every**
year in this country that are never solved? And why? Because they're
motiveless. The perfect murder is the motiveless murder.

Brian That's easy to say. Something would be bound to go wrong somewhere.

Gerry You've been reading too many thrillers. Look, I know you don't
want any part of it, but just as a game, let me prove it to you.

Brian lays the revolver aside

Brian All right. Try.

Gerry To begin with, nobody knows I came here tonight. Correct?

Brian As far as I know.

Gerry And nobody will see me go. So we've never met, which rules out
the possibility of collusion between us. Point one established.

Brian Wait a minute. How did you get here—to Dorking, I mean?

Gerry By commuter train from London. Packed and everybody buried
behind the evening papers. Complete anonymity.

Brian Where were you before that?

Gerry Abroad. Italy. I arrived at Dover this morning.

Brian And after?

Gerry I got a lift on a lorry to London.

Brian Then the driver would know you again.

Gerry So what? A hitch-hiker isn't necessarily a murderer.

Brian Do your parents know you're back in England?

Gerry No.

Brian When did you last write to them?

Gerry I sent them a picture postcard six months ago.

Brian Saying you were coming home?

Gerry No. Saying I was staying abroad. I intended to at that time. Satisfied? You can be. I worked it all out while I was upstairs.

Brian No, I want to think. (*He rises and puts the revolver back in the
desk*)

Gerry So you are considering the idea?

Brian No, I'm not! I'm just seeing how it could be possible to do it. You
came in here—you sat over there. I got you something to eat. While I
was out of the room you touched various things. You put on the record
player. That means your fingerprints are all over the place.

Gerry Didn't I hear something about a daily?

Brian Yes, but she's not very thorough.

Gerry Then a spot of housework from you would be required.

Brian All right, say any fingerprints are taken care of. You still haven't
told me how it would be done.

Gerry What do you make the time?

Brian (*surprised*) Time? (*He looks at his watch*) Eleven-ten. Why?

Gerry It's getting late. Are you usually in bed before this?

Brian Mostly. Unless I'm out for the evening, I watch TV in the bedroom.

Gerry Then I'd put out the lights and draw the curtains, if I were you.

Brian This house can barely be seen from either side.

Gerry All the same, we wouldn't want some nosey neighbour saying you were keeping extra late hours a few nights before it happened. It mightn't mean anything, but it pays to act normally.

Brian puts out the lights and draws the curtains. Then moves again to the light switch

No, not the main ones. Just the small lamp will do.

Brian switches on a small lamp on the desk

Right. Now slip upstairs, put on the light in your bedroom and draw the curtains. In a few minutes, go up again and put the light out. Then it'll seem you'll have gone to bed.

Brian (*shrugging*) All right. It's your game.

Brian goes off upstairs

Gerry moves to the desk, takes out a handkerchief and opens the drawer. Inside is a photograph of Sheila. He takes it out, holding the frame by the handkerchief, and studies it. Then he puts it back, closing the drawer

Brian returns

Brian All set.

Gerry Good. Then we come to how it would be done. The first part involves you.

Brian You said I wouldn't be involved!

Gerry Not actively. Only your movements. Are you on a job tomorrow?

Brian Not until Friday. Tomorrow I take back the car I brought home tonight and write my report.

Gerry What do you do Friday?

Brian I collect a Marina for testing.

Gerry (*pacing, thinking*) Where do you pick it up?

Brian Croydon. About mid-day.

Gerry And you drive these cars—how far?

Brian Depends. A couple of hundred miles. Two-fifty sometimes.

Gerry Then you bring them back here, write your report, and take them back next day?

Brian Yes.

Gerry That's fine. Only on Friday—assuming I did this—you wouldn't bring the car back here. You'd stay somewhere overnight. I take it you could fake some mechanical trouble? Something that couldn't immediately be put right?

Brian Easily.

Gerry Good. So you break down about a hundred and fifty miles from here. Have you got a road map?

Brian Small scale?

Gerry Doesn't matter.

Brian (*finding a map in the magazine rack*) This do?

Gerry You handle it. Turn up Croydon.

Brian does so, and holds the map between them

Where would you drive the car to test it properly from there?
Brian I'd probably go out to Guildford . . .
Gerry A good long run, mind.
Brian On to Winchester. Could go as far as Salisbury.
Gerry Make it Salisbury. So at Salisbury you break down. Got that?
Brian Yes.
Gerry And book into a hotel for the night. All right, I've finished with
    that.

Brian puts the map away

Now, if we were really going ahead with this, the next thing I should
want you to do is to make a phone call to Sheila.
Brian Sheila? What for?
Gerry To make sure she was here on Friday evening. You can't have a
    murder without a victim.
Brian But—what reason would I give?
Gerry Didn't I hear something about her collecting some clothes?
Brian Yes.
Gerry There's your reason. You ask her to come and collect them on
    Friday evening. Let's say eight o'clock when it's really dark.
Brian She'd be sure to want to come during the day!
Gerry Ah, then you say you'd rather she didn't because Mrs Thing'll be
    here. You haven't told her anything about the divorce, and she's bound
    to be curious.
Brian Suppose she wanted to come earlier?
Gerry Eight o'clock, you tell her, is the time she can be quite certain of
    not seeing you. And after tonight you're sure she'd rather not see you
    again. The point is, I have to know exactly when she'd be here.
Brian If she said eight she'd be here on the dot.
Gerry Good. Well, go on. Phone her.
Brian But—we were only talking!
Gerry I know. But it's all part of the game. I couldn't tell you how the
    rest works unless I knew for certain she was coming.
Brian I don't see it's necessary to do this.
Gerry What harm can it do? She's got to collect her things some time,
    and you might as well be out of her way on Friday as any other day.

Brian takes up the phone, then hesitates

Brian She may not be home yet.
Gerry Try her anyway. I'll go and put your bedroom light out.

Brian dials

> *Gerry goes off upstairs*

After a few rings Brian is about to hang up, when he hears a voice

Brian Sheila?... Yes, Brian. Have you just got in?... It's about collecting the rest of your things. I wonder if you could make it Friday evening about eight?... Tomorrow? No, not tomorrow ... Well, I shall be home early, and I didn't think you'd be particularly anxious to find me here. On Friday, I'm picking up a car much later ... Yes, I know the daytime would suit you better, but Mrs Abbott'll be here, and she's bound to want to know why she hasn't seen you lately ... I just told her you were staying in town ... You'll make it Friday then, at eight? Thanks—thanks very much—and Sheila ... I'm sorry. (*He replaces the receiver*)

Gerry appears on the stairs. He is dressed in a white mackintosh of Sheila's and wears a wig that is an exact replica of her long blonde hair

Brian, having replaced the phone, has his back to the stairs. Gerry speaks in a slightly higher voice

Gerry How are you, Brian?

Brian turns, and knocks the telephone off the desk

Brian Christ!
Gerry (*chuckling*) It's only me.
Brian (*furiously*) What the hell do you think you're playing at! You frightened the life out of me. I thought for the moment it was Sheila. (*He picks up the phone*)
Gerry Good, isn't it? I saw these things when I was upstairs before, and they gave me the idea.
Brian Take them off, for God's sake!
Gerry All right. (*He takes off the wig and coat and lays them on a chair putting the wig under the mackintosh*) What did she say?
Brian She's coming at eight on Friday. And now I think you'd better go. I'm getting fed up with this charade.
Gerry But we're just coming to the interesting part. You must let me tell you.
Brian Make it short then.
Gerry (*taking his arm and leading him away from the light and into the shadow*) If we were really doing this thing, my dear Brian, this is what would happen ...

The Lights fade to a Blackout. The use of suitable music during this flash-forward sequence is most effective

During the Blackout Gerry and Brian slip out, Gerry taking his hold-all with him. The wig and the mackintosh are still where Gerry left them

When the Lights come up, the room is empty

Sheila appears at the top of the stairs, dressed as before, and carrying a fairly heavy suitcase, and her handbag. She descends the stairs and places the case by the front door, then turns to go upstairs again. As she does so there is a knock at the front door. She hesitates, descends again and opens the door. Gerry is outside, carrying his hold-all, and wearing his anorak

Sheila Yes?

Gerry (*at his most ingratiating*) Good evening. I'm terribly sorry to bother you—I wondered—I'm on a walking tour, you see—and I wondered if you could direct me. Is there a Youth Hostel or a Y.M.C.A. round here?

Sheila I'm sorry. I really don't know. If you go back to the main road, I'm sure you'll find someone who can tell you.

Gerry I did hope to. There just wasn't anyone about. And as I was at the bottom of your drive . . .

Sheila I'm sorry. I just don't know. Now, I'm afraid you must excuse me . . .

Gerry I know. The telephone book. Could I look in that. It wouldn't take a minute.

Sheila Well, I—oh, very well.

She moves from the door. Gerry enters

There it is.

Gerry (*opening the telephone book*) Don't let me keep you from anything you're doing.

Sheila That's all right.

Gerry Here it is. Y.M.C.A., Walmer Road. Is that far from here?

Sheila About two miles.

Gerry Two miles!

Sheila Yes.

Gerry Oh, dear, I think I shall have to doss down at the police station if its nearer.

Sheila It is. (*She laughs*)

Gerry Unless—is that your car outside?

Sheila Yes. Why?

Gerry I know you'll think this an awful nerve, but—(*he indicates the case*) —you seem to be going somewhere. You couldn't give me a lift, could you?

Sheila I'm right in the middle of packing.

Gerry I could wait. I'd willingly pay for the petrol.

Sheila Don't be silly. Only it would be very inconvenient. I'm not nearly finished here.

Gerry Never mind. Sorry to have troubled you. (*He moves to the door*)

Sheila Oh, all right. I'll run you into the town. I can be there and back in ten minutes.

Gerry That's most awfully good of you.

Sheila I'll just get my coat. Sit down.

Sheila goes upstairs

The moment Sheila has gone Gerry takes a pair of dark gloves from his pocket and slips them on. He goes to the mackintosh and takes the belt from it, rolling it up and hiding it behind his back. He then places the wig on top of the mackintosh. He hears Sheila coming, and sits down

Sheila enters, wearing her coat

Just my bag, for my car keys. (*She goes to her handbag*)

Gerry (*rising, moving to the wig*) Is this yours?

Sheila Yes. How on earth did that get down here. I was looking for it upstairs.

Gerry It's marvellous, isn't it? Just like your own hair.

Sheila Yes, I had it made specially. I'll just put it in my case. I don't want to forget it.

Sheila goes to the case by the door, and kneels by it. Gerry comes softly behind her, and with a swift movement, slips the belt over her head. Sheila struggles, but he presses down on her, tightening the belt. The struggle is quite prolonged, but eventually Sheila lies still. Gerry straightens up. The telephone rings suddenly. Gerry stands listening. It rings six times then stops. Gerry switches off the lights and opens the front door

Gerry lifts Sheila and carries her outside, returning after a few moments

Gerry goes to the window and draws the curtains, then switches on the lights. He goes to the mackintosh, threads the belt through the loops and, taking off his anorak, puts the mackintosh on. He picks up the wig from where it has fallen and, going to the mirror, puts it on carefully. He stuffs his anorak into his hold-all, picks up Sheila's handbag, finds her car keys, and takes them out. Slipping the bag over his arm, he picks up the suitcase and hold-all, switches off the lights, and opens the front door

Gerry goes out, closing the door behind him

A car is heard to start up and drive off

The Lights fade to a Blackout

During the Blackout the wig and mackintosh are replaced. Brian and Gerry take up their positions as before

The Lights come up as previously

Gerry When I take her out to the car I put her on the floor behind the front seats. Then I drive to a quiet spot about five miles from here, and leave the car in a lay-by. I take off the wig and mackintosh, put them in her suitcase and disappear. She may be found next morning—she may not be found for days. But either way I shall be miles off, and you'll be in the clear.

Brian There'd be nothing to tell the police anything?

Gerry Nothing. She won't have been raped or robbed. It's a completely motiveless murder. Well, that's the set-up. Now you question me and see if you can break it down,

Brian All right. To begin with, why the disguise?

Gerry It's a precaution. If the car should be seen by someone as it turns into the main road, it will appear your wife was driving it.

Brian But I don't see the point of it. If you were going to kill her, why not do it here and go?

Gerry Would you want the police swarming all over the place—asking you questions—finally discovering she was packing up to leave you? They would, you know. This way, with only one suitcase with her, she could just have been going away for a week or so.

Brian And the assumption would be that she picked up a hitch-hiker who killed her?

Gerry Yes. Anything else?

Brian Yes. Supposing she wouldn't let you into the house?

Gerry You would have given me a key, just in case. Have you got a spare one?

Brian There's one in here. (*He moves to the desk and opens a drawer. For some reason, he does not close it*) The wig and the mackintosh. How could you be sure they'd be in the right place?

Gerry You'd put them there. In fact, you'd leave them where they are now.

Brian I see.

Gerry You haven't asked me one important thing. Who was phoning?

Brian No, I meant to. Who?

Gerry You.

Brian Me? Where would I be phoning from?

Gerry Your hotel in Salisbury. You've checked in after the breakdown. Then, naturally you ring your wife and tell her you won't be home.

Brian I take it I'd make a big play of this phoning?

Gerry Of course. For instance, you'd use the call-box in the foyer, so you'd have to get change from the bar and ask how much you need to phone Dorking. You'd be well away from the murder zone, anyway, but all this would be making your alibi cast-iron.

Brian And the time I should phone? Is that important?

Gerry Very. You'd ring at exactly a quarter past eight, and let the phone ring six times. Exactly six. Then I would know it was you. (*He replaces the Coke can on the bar*) And, by the way, there's something I should need to know. What kind of car does your wife drive?

Brian Fiat.

Gerry Automatic?

Brian No, manual.

Gerry So that wouldn't present any problems. (*He stretches*) Well, there you are. That's the little Murder Game—all cut and dried. (*He moves to his hold-all and picks it up*) Thanks for a very nice evening.

Brian Wait a minute. There was something you didn't clear up.

Gerry Oh. What was that?

Brian What you would expect to get out of this.

Gerry I've told you. The thrill of a lifetime. The satisfaction of committing the perfect murder.

Brian I think you suggested this for another reason.

Gerry You could add that I don't like women.

Brian I suspected that, but it's not what I meant. I think there might be blackmail at the end of it.

Gerry What for?

Brian Money, of course! You'd know I'd be coming into a fortune if my wife died. What would there be to stop you coming back and bleeding me white?

Gerry Nothing, I suppose. Except I don't see why you couldn't trust me.

Brian How the hell could I trust you when I don't even know who you are?

Gerry starts to speak

Oh, I know you told me your name, but that could be false, for a start.

Gerry All right, here's my passport. (*He takes it from his hip pocket*) Satisfied?

Brian What's your background?

Gerry Public school. You don't have to know which one. My parents are rich but they don't support me, and I've never been short of money in my life. Is that enough?

Brian No. You've more or less admitted you make your money in illegal ways. I could still be one of your victims.

Gerry (*sighing*) You really are difficult. (*He takes a thick envelope from his hold-all and holds it out*) Will *that* convince you?

Brian What is it?

Gerry Open it.

Brian opens the envelope and takes out several thick wads of notes

Brian God almighty!

Gerry You see, I don't need your money. I should think, at this moment, I'm worth far more than you are.

Brian How much is here?

Gerry Three thousand—all in used fivers.

Brian Three thousand! Where the devil did you get this kind of money? Have you just done a robbery?

Gerry No, I earned it.

Brian You don't earn an amount like this honestly, and in cash!

Gerry Not *honestly*, perhaps, but you *can* earn it.

Brian How?

Gerry I made it running money.

Brian Running money?

Gerry That's what they call it. In nearly every country in the world, millionaires are trying to get their money out—tax reasons, or just inflation. All you have to do is take a letter of credit and lodge it in a Swiss bank, and you get a percentage. I did it three times from Italy before the Italian police started to get wise to the dodge.

Brian And this is your percentage?

Gerry Yes.

Brian You make me feel I was born yesterday. (*He hands the money back*)
Gerry Most of your generation were.
Brian Have you got a record of any sort?
Gerry Not of any sort. Clean as a new-born babe, is Gerry. So you don't
want to go on with the game?
Brian I don't want any part of it.
Gerry O.K.
Brian I've never seen you and we've never talked like this. Understood?
Gerry Of course, of course. But it was an interesting discussion, don't
you think? (*He moves near to the drawer where the key is*) Only I would
ask you one favour.
Brian What's that?
Gerry Don't use the idea yourself. After all, it *is* mine, and I may want to
use it some day.

*Gerry quietly takes the key from the drawer. Brian sees him, but deliberately
turns away. Gerry moves to the door*

Brian You're not sleeping in the summerhouse. (*It is a statement*)
Gerry Of course not. I'm on my way to heaven knows where. (*He reaches
the door*) Thanks for the hospitality. (*He opens the door, then turns*)
You know, I think it would be a good idea if you *did* stay at Salisbury
on Friday night. After all, one never knows what may happen.

Gerry smiles and goes out, closing the door

*Brian waits till the door shuts, then moves to the open drawer where the key
was. He looks down into it*

The Lights fade slowly to a Blackout

*When the Lights come up again it is to show the window curtains undrawn
and the interior lighting on. It is Friday, about eight o'clock in the evening*

*The wig and mackintosh are lying where they were before. The record-
player is playing softly the tune Gerry first put on*

*After a moment, Sheila enters down the stairs carrying a suitcase, which
she places by the front door*

*As she turns to go upstairs again, she sees a photograph of Brian. She picks it
up and looks at it, then moves towards her suitcase as if to put it in. However,
she changes her mind, and replaces it where it was. Opening her handbag
which is over her arm, she takes from it a letter, which she props up against
the photograph. She crosses to the stairs and is about to ascend when there
is a knock at the door. She frowns, hesitates, then descends, pausing to
switch off the record-player. She crosses to the door and opens it*

*Gerry is outside, wearing his anorak and carrying his hold-all. He is wearing
gloves*

Sheila Yes?

Gerry Good evening. I'm terribly sorry to bother you, but——

Sheila If you're a Jehovah's Witness, I'm sorry, I haven't time to listen.

Gerry Oh, no, I'm not. Nothing like that. I'm on a walking tour, you see, and I'm stuck for somewhere to sleep tonight. I wondered if you could direct me. Is there a Youth Hostel or a Y.M.C.A. round here?

Sheila I really don't know. If you go back to the main road, I'm sure you'll be able to find someone who can tell you.

Gerry I did hope to. There just wasn't anyone about. Then I saw your light up here.

Sheila I'm sorry. I simply don't know. Now you must excuse me. I'm terribly busy.

Gerry Do you think one of your neighbours might know?

Sheila Possibly. Why not ask? Now, if you don't mind . . .

Gerry I know! The telephone book. Could I look in that? I won't be a minute, really.

Sheila Oh—oh, very well.

Reluctantly she lets him enter. She precedes him and gives him the phone book

There you are.

Gerry Thanks awfully

Sheila stays watching him

Don't let me keep you from whatever you're doing. I shan't pinch anything. (*He smiles disarmingly*)

Sheila I can spare a few moments.

Gerry turns over the pages of the book

Wouldn't you find it easier if you took your gloves off?

Gerry My hands are so cold. I can manage.

Sheila's suspicions are aroused, though she does not know quite why

Sheila Would you like a drink?

Gerry Oh, thanks. If you've got a Coke.

Sheila Wouldn't you prefer something warmer?

Gerry Oh, no, I don't drink. A Coke would be fine.

Sheila All right.

As she crosses to the bar she makes a slight detour to the desk, and, her back to Gerry, takes the revolver from its pigeon-hole. She moves behind the bar and searches, placing the revolver behind a bottle

That's odd. I can't find any.

Gerry It doesn't matter, really.

Sheila But we had several cans. I can't think where its gone. It's not like my husband to touch the stuff.

Gerry Don't bother about it. I've found the address. Walmer Road.

Sheila Good.

Gerry Is that far from here?

Sheila Quite a way. About two miles. We're a bit out of the town here. Still, I think you may be able to pick up a bus along the main road.

Gerry You've been awfully kind. Thank you.

Sheila Not at all. (*She opens the front door*) Sorry I couldn't do more.

Gerry (*pausing*) Well—actually you can.

Sheila Oh?

Gerry Is that your car outside?

Sheila Yes.

Gerry I know you'll think I've got a frightful nerve, but I really am very tired. If I waited, could you give me a lift there?

Sheila I'm in the middle of packing.

Gerry I don't mind waiting.

Sheila I shall be another hour at least.

Gerry Oh. Well, never mind.

Sheila (*relenting*) All right, I'll run you into the town. I can be there and back in a few minutes.

Gerry It's very kind of you. (*He makes to come back into the room*)

Sheila (*barring his way*) Wait in the car while I get my coat.

Gerry Is there anything I can carry out for you?

Sheila No, thanks.

Gerry goes out

Sheila shuts the door, and stands for a moment looking worried. Then she runs upstairs quickly

Sheila exits

The handle of the door is turned, but it does not open. Then a key is softly inserted into the lock

Gerry opens the front door and enters. He slips the key back into his pocket and closes the door quietly. He glances upstairs, then moves swiftly to the white mackintosh, takes the belt out and places the wig on top of the mackintosh. He noiselessly moves towards the kitchen door and exits

Sheila appears on the stairs, wearing her coat and carrying her handbag

She goes to the bar, picks up the revolver, and puts it in her handbag. She is moving to the door when she sees the wig and mackintosh. She picks them up and moves with them to her suitcase

Gerry enters from the kitchen, the belt in both hands

Sheila kneels and opens the suitcase. He comes noiselessly behind her. As she goes to put the wig and mackintosh in, he slips the belt over her head and pulls it tight. Sheila struggles, but he bears down on her, until eventually she lies still. He rises, panting, switches off the lights, draws the curtains, then opens the front door

Lifting Sheila, Gerry carries her outside

The room is empty for a moment or two

Gerry returns. He turns on the lights and threads the belt through the mackintosh. Taking off his anorak he puts on the mackintosh, then goes to the mirror and puts on the wig. He stuffs the anorak into his hold-all

Gerry (*muttering*) Car keys. (*He finds Sheila's handbag and opens it, discovering, to his surprise, the revolver. He weighs it in his hand for a moment, then replaces it in the pigeon-hole of the desk. He finds the car keys and closes the handbag. Looking carefully round, he is about to go to the door when he sees the envelope propped against Brian's photograph. He picks it up, then opens and reads it. A smile spreads over his face. He replaces it in the envelope and slips it into his jeans pocket. He moves to the front door, picks up the hold-all and suitcase and switches off the lights. Then he goes to open the front door*)

The telephone rings. Gerry stops and listens. It rings six times, then stops

Gerry smiles, opens the front door and goes out, closing it behind him

A moment later, a car is heard to start and drive away. The Lights fade to a Blackout, as—

the CURTAIN *falls*

ACT II

Scene 1

The same. Six months later. Morning

June Maitland, a very pretty, very nice and intelligent girl of about twenty-six (not at all the bitch Sheila described) is sitting at the desk typing. She finishes the sheet, pulls it from the typewriter, and lays it aside with the carbon. She covers the typewriter, puts it in a corner out of the way, and puts her chair back in its place. She goes into the kitchen and returns a moment later with a cloth which she spreads over the dining-table. Going again into the kitchen, she returns with cutlery, and proceeds to lay the table. Then she goes once more into the kitchen

A car approaches and pulls up outside. After a moment, the front door opens and Brian enters. He is cheerful and relaxed. He carries Sheila's suitcase from the previous act

Brian Anybody home? (*He puts down the case*)

June enters, wiping her hands on a cloth

June You're back sooner than I expected.
Brian Yes, they didn't keep me long, thank God. (*They kiss not passionately, but affectionately*) You smell of cooking.
June Nasty?
Brian No, nice—very nice. I'm glad to see you've not been idling while I've been out.
June I've typed your car report as well. (*She fetches the typed sheet*) See?
Brian That's good. I can get it off. When did you learn to type so well?
June While I was "resting". I had plenty of time, believe me. Did you want to post it right away? I've typed an envelope. (*She brings an envelope from the desk*)
Brian Have I time before lunch?
June Half an hour at least.
Brian Then I think I will. I've been a bit erratic with my reports lately, having to go down to the police station so much. This'll put me in their good books again.
June (*seeing the case he has set down*) Is that Sheila's suitcase?
Brian Yes. They said I could take it away now. I suppose they kept it all this time, hoping to get something from it.
June Poor Brian. It's been a beastly time for you.
Brian Not too pleasant. (*Moving to the bar*) Drink?
June Just a small one.

Brian The usual?
June Please. (*She sits*)
Brian (*searching*) There doesn't seem to be any red wine.
June Oh, no, of course! I put the last of it into the beef stroganoff.
Brian It couldn't be in a better place. Sherry do?
June Yes, fine. Is it all over now, then?
Brian I think so. They don't seem to have any clue as to who could have done it. (*He goes to her with her drink*)
June Thanks. But I suppose they'll always go on looking?
Brian (*moving back to the bar*) Yes, I don't think they ever really drop a case. Though I should think any lead they ever had was as cold as charity by now. (*He pours himself a whisky*)
June Oh, darling, wouldn't it have been awful if you'd have been implicated?
Brian (*sharply*) How could I have been?
June Well, I mean if you'd been anywhere near where it happened.
Brian Yes, I see . . . Yes, of course, if the car hadn't broken down I'd have been on my way back.
June So it was providential, really. Though, on the other hand, if you *had* come back it might never have happened.
Brian How do you mean?
June Well, if you'd got back while she was still here, you might have talked a bit, and she might never have met this man who did it.
Brian Instead, someone else would have.
June Yes, I suppose so.
Brian (*moving to her*) Don't you ever stop to pick up a hitch-hiker.
June (*laughing*) I'd be far too nervous.
Brian Promise me.
June I promise. (*She rises, putting her glass on the bar*) Would you like me to unpack that case?
Brian It's a rotten job for you.
June Not so bad for me as for you. I'll put the things in the wardrobe. Then you can decide what you want to do with them.
Brian Oh, chuck them all out. (*He sits*)
June But, darling, that's terribly wasteful. She had some lovely things. In fact, if it wouldn't upset you too much, I'd like to have some of them.
Brian I don't want you wearing Sheila's things!
June But some are nearly new . . .
Brian No! Please, June, I'd rather you didn't. I can afford to buy you new ones.
June All right.
Brian If you've got any friends in the profession who'd like to have them, give them to them by all means.
June They'll leap at them.
Brian (*taking several travel brochures from his pocket*) By the way, I got these at the travel bureau on my way back.
June What for?

Brian Well, I thought—now the affair's as nearly cleared up as it's ever likely to be, we might go abroad for a bit.
June That would be marvellous. When were you thinking of?
Brian As soon as possible. We could get married first—after all, it *is* nearly six months—then be off by the end of this month.
June (*dismayed*) But, darling, you've forgotten.
Brian What?
June I can't. Not at that time.
Brian Why not?
June My film is coming up then.
Brian Couldn't you drop out of it? Its only a bit part.
June But it is an important film. I might be seen by somebody.
Brian I don't care if nobody ever sees you but me.
June But *I* do. It's the first decent break I've ever had. Can't we wait till it's finished? I shall only be needed for about three weeks.
Brian I shall hate being here without you. Would it be possible for me to come with you?
June Oh, darling, you'd be bored stiff. It's all hanging about, and nobody ever seems to do anything. Besides, there's your work.
Brian Yes, there's that, of course.
June It won't seem so very long, honestly. We could get away by the end of September at the latest.
Brian All right. If you say so.
June You really are the *nicest*! (*She kisses him on top of the head*) Now you'd better go and post your letter while I do the rest of the lunch. Don't stop at the pub on your way back.
Brian (*rising*) Not even a quickie?
June (*going with him to the door*) Make sure it is, then. You've only twenty minutes. Lunch is one o'clock sharp.
Brian One o'clock it is.

Brian exits by the front door with the letter

June gives him a wave, then closes the door. Brian's car is heard to start and drive off. June is about to return to the kitchen when the sight of the suitcase stops her. She picks it up, brings it to a chair and tries to open it. It is locked. She then sees the keys are tied to the handle, and unlocks the case, and opens it. On top are the white mackintosh and the long fair wig. She takes the wig out and looks at it admiringly. There is a knock at the front door. June puts the wig back on top of the mackintosh but does not close the case. She goes to the door and opens it

Gerry is outside, dressed as before, and carrying his hold-all

Gerry (*with great charm*) Good morning. Is Mr Hamilton in?
June No, I'm sorry. He's gone down to the post. You've just missed him.
Gerry Oh, what a pity. Will he be long?
June Not if he values his peace of mind, he won't.

Gerry looks at her inquiringly

    Lunch is at one.

Gerry I see.

June Would you like to come back this afternoon? He'll be in for the rest of the day.

Gerry Well, I'd rather see him this morning, if it's possible.

June Then you'd better come in and wait.

Gerry Would you mind?

June Of course not, so long as you don't mind me darting in and out of the kitchen.

Gerry (*entering the room*) Don't take any notice of me.

June (*closing the door*) Do sit down. Are you a friend of Brian's?

Gerry Not really. We only met once. He was very kind to me. (*He sits*)

June In what way?

Gerry Like a fool I stepped out in front of his car one day. It was only by a miracle he missed me. He was awfully decent about it, although it was entirely my fault.

June Yes, he would be.

Gerry Still, you know what a terrific driver he is . . .

June Yes.

Gerry Being his wife.

June I'm not—his wife.

Gerry Oh, I'm so sorry. Do forgive me. I thought you must be Sheila.

June No. Would you like a drink?

Gerry That's very kind of you.

June What would you like? (*She goes to the bar*) We've got most things.

Gerry A Coke, if you have it.

June Yes, I think so. Yes, we have. (*She opens a can and pours it into a glass*) Didn't you meet Sheila when you met Brian?

Gerry No, she was away. I think Brian said she was staying in town.

June (*unthinkingly*) Oh, so it was when they . . . (*She stops*)

Gerry I beg your pardon?

June Nothing. (*She hands him the glass*)

Gerry Thank you. Is she away at the moment?

June No. Obviously you haven't heard.

Gerry Heard what?

June She's dead.

Gerry Dead? But how terrible. She couldn't have been very old.

June Thirty-four. (*She sits*)

Gerry I can hardly believe it. Was it a very sudden illness?

June It wasn't an illness. She was—murdered.

Gerry Murdered!

June About six months ago. It happened in her car. She must have stopped on the road to pick up someone who was thumbing a lift, and he killed her. That's what the police think, anyway.

Gerry What a dreadful thing! I suppose it was robbery as well as murder?

June No, that was the odd thing about it. Nothing was taken, although she was carrying quite a lot of money. It wasn't rape, either, or anything like that. Just an apparently motiveless murder.

Gerry Poor Brian. It must have been a terrible shock for him.

June It was. He was away the evening it happened. He knew nothing about it until the police phoned him. (*Pause*) You must think it rather strange my being here with him.

Gerry No, why should I? As far as I'm concerned, you might be his house-keeper.

June No, I'm not that. I'm staying with Brian for a bit. We're going to be married. (*She rises, going to the bar to pour another sherry*) It isn't as heartless as it may sound. We did know each other before.

Gerry I see.

June (*turning to look at him*) I wonder if Brian may have mentioned you to me. What's your name?

Gerry I doubt if he'd even remember it. I only came in here the once. I'm Gerry Stephens.

June (*holding out her hand*) June Maitland. How do you do?

Gerry (*rising; shaking hands*) How do you do?

June Another Coke—or something shorter? (*She rises*)

Gerry Nothing more, thanks. (*He looks at the suitcase*) Have I interrupted your packing? Are you going away somewhere?

June No. That isn't my suitcase. It's Sheila's.

Gerry Mrs Hamilton's?

June Yes. The police have just released it. They've kept it until now, hoping, I suppose, to get some sort of clue from it. Brian brought it back this morning. I ought to put it away somewhere. It's such a dreadful reminder to him, but clothes fascinate me. I was just going to have a look at them.

Gerry (*looking into the suitcase*) What a wonderful wig that is!

June Yes, isn't it? (*She picks it up and looks at it admiringly*) Real hair. It must have cost a fortune.

Gerry Is that how she wore her hair? Or perhaps you didn't know her?

June (*with recollections*) We only met once. Yes, I seem to remember this is how she wore it.

Gerry It would suit you.

June It's not my colour.

Gerry I think you'd look marvellous blonde.

June I have thought of going fair. I mentioned it to Brian once, but he hated the idea. I suppose it was because it was Sheila's colour.

Gerry Try it on.

June Oh, no, I couldn't.

Gerry You'd look lovely in it.

June No, really. (*She goes to put it back in the suitcase*)

Gerry May I?

June You?

Gerry Just for fun. (*Without waiting for permission, he puts it on. As before, it suits him admirably*) How do you like me?

June (*laughing*) You look marvellous in it! You ought to do a drag act.

Gerry I used to act all the women in plays at school. (*He takes off the wig and hands it to her*)

June Are you in the Profession?

Gerry Profession?

June Mine. I'm an actress. Well, sort of.

Gerry No, I'm just a wanderer. I like to go where I like—do what I please. Luckily, I can turn my hand to most things—even cooking.

June I should think that would get you a job anywhere. Especially here.

Gerry Oh, rubbish. I'm sure you can cook beautifully.

June (*laying the wig back in the suitcase, and picking up her sherry again*) I do try awfully hard, but I have to keep my nose buried in the cookery book all the time. Brian's terribly gallant. He pretends to enjoy my cooking, but he'll fare far better when I've gone abroad. (*She sits*)

Gerry Are you going away? (*He sits*)

June Yes, shortly—to Spain. I've got a rather important little bit in a film coming up in September.

Gerry I'm sorry. I was awfully rude.

June Rude? How?

Gerry You're probably famous, and I ought to have known your name.

June (*smiling*) Even a film fanatic isn't likely to know my name. I never get more than bit parts in films and the occasional supporting part in a play.

Gerry Still, this film is important?

June To me, yes. You see, it might easily lead to something better.

Gerry Dare I ask the name of the film?

June No, I mustn't reveal it. Not that it'll be the same by the time it's shown. But the director is just about the tops, so you can imagine how thrilled I am about it.

Gerry What part are you playing?

June An English girl tourist. The male lead is a Spanish guide, and she's one of the people he swindles. I only have a scene with the Spanish police, but at least it's more dialogue than I've ever had before.

Gerry You're going to need that wig.

June Why?

Gerry Well, you can't possibly play an English girl in Spain with dark hair.

June I suppose I shall have to go blonde. But they'll see to that.

Gerry (*rising and picking up the wig*) See how you look now.

June (*taking the wig*) You tempt me. (*She rises*)

Gerry Are you supposed to be rich in the film?

June Oh, loaded. Why?

Gerry Because that colour goes marvellously with mink. You must make them give you a mink coat to wear.

June There's a mink coat in Sheila's wardrobe. I've been longing to try it on.

Gerry Try them both while Brian's not here. Go on. It can't do any harm. He'll never know.

June No. I'm going to put them away, out of temptation's reach. (*She closes the case*)
Gerry Can I carry that up for you?
June No, thanks. (*She takes the case to the stairs*) It's not heavy. (*She puts it down*) But I must see to the oven first.
Gerry Let me. What do you want done?
June Would you put it down to three-fifty?
Gerry Will do. Anything else?
June Well, if you could put the saucepan on for the rice. It's on the draining-board.
Gerry Right. As good as done.
June Thanks. (*She picks up the case and ascends the stairs*)
Gerry Shall I put on some music?
June If you like.

June exits upstairs

Gerry goes into the kitchen and returns almost at once, tying on an apron

He goes to the record-player, sees the disc he wants is not on it, then looks through the records. He finds "the" tune and puts it on

Gerry exits to the kitchen

The music starts to sound softly. A clatter of saucepans is heard from the kitchen

Brian enters from the front door, looking annoyed. He carries the letter, which he throws on to the bar, then pours himself a drink

June appears on the stairs, dressed in the wig and Sheila's mink coat

(*running downstairs*) I succumbed to temptation. (*She sees Brian and stops dismayed*)

Brian turns and sees her. His glass overturns and he staggers back against the bar

What's the matter? (*Coming to him*) Brian!
Brian What the hell do you think you're doing? I told you to leave those things alone!
June I'm sorry—I didn't mean you to see . . . What brought you back so quickly?
Brian (*recovering*) Picked up a puncture half-way down the drive. Then the jack wouldn't work.
June I'll get you another drink.
Brian I can get my own drink! Take those bloody things off!
June All right. I'm sorry.

June pulls off the wig and starts upstairs. Brian pours a drink with a shaking hand

Brian And get rid of them like I told you! (*He becomes conscious of the music*) Did you put that tune on?

June Tune? No, I expect it was your friend. He's waiting to see you.

She runs upstairs. Brian crosses to stairs switching off player on the way

Brian What friend?

June exits. Gerry enters from the kitchen

Gerry Your best friend, of course. Me.

Brian turns and stares at him

How are you, Brian?

Brian Where the hell did you spring from?

Gerry The kitchen. I was just putting on the rice for lunch.

Brian I don't mean that and you know it. How did you get here?

Gerry I walked up your drive.

Brian I didn't see you.

Gerry I know you didn't. I heard you coming and nipped behind a tree. Careful, you're spilling that. Shall I get you another?

Brian What are you doing here?

Gerry Paying you a friendly visit.

Brian What for?

Gerry My dear Brian, one doesn't pay friendly visits *for* anything. I just thought I'd like to see how you were getting on. And you mustn't blame June for what happened just now. It was really my idea.

Brian (*moving to the bar*) I can imagine. Just the sort of beastly sadistic thing you would think of.

Gerry Well, I could see that she was longing to try them on. After all, you weren't expected back so soon.

Brian I'd bet even money you knew I was coming back.

Gerry Well, I must admit I did see you pick up that puncture. (*Smiling*) You've been unlucky with your cars lately, haven't you?

Brian What do you mean? (*He pours another drink*)

Gerry You had a breakdown just before Sheila was killed, didn't you?

Brian I don't know what you're talking about. I've got nothing to say to you, and now you've seen me you can be on your way.

Gerry (*holding up a finger*) Wait. I think the rice is boiling. Excuse me, while I go and turn it down.

Gerry exits to the kitchen

Brian fumes

June appears on the stairs and comes down

Brian (*moving to her and speaking quietly*) How did he get in here?

June He knocked at the door and asked for you. He said he was a friend of yours, so I asked him in. Wasn't it all right?

Brian I'd rather you hadn't, that's all.

June But, Brian, he thinks the world of you! He told me how you met, and how decent you were to him. He seems very innocuous to me.

Brian Innocuous! What's he been saying to you?

June Nothing in particular. We talked about my film, and he told me he was one of those people who wander about everywhere, doing odd jobs. Did you know he can even cook?

Brian Did he say anything about me?

June Only what I told you. At first he thought I was Sheila—I suppose you must have mentioned her to him. He was terribly shocked when I told him about her death.

Brian You're sure he said nothing more?

June No. What more could he have said? He told me you met only the once. That *was* all, wasn't it?

Brian (*moving away from her*) Yes, and it was quite enough.

June (*following*) Darling, aren't you being a bit prejudiced about him? He's not much more than a kid, and one can see how he admires you.

Brian without answering, goes to bar and refills his glass

How long is it since you first met him?

Brian Six months.

June Well, you can hardly say he's made a nuisance of himself, can you? Let's give him lunch, then send him on his way. Or do you want to change the wheel first?

Brian No.

Gerry enters from kitchen, untying the apron

Gerry (*handing the apron to June*) Over to you. Everything's under control. There's a kettle of boiling water ready for you to pour through the rice when its finished.

June What would I do that for?

Gerry (*clicking his tongue*) You haven't read your cookery books very thoroughly. That gets all the starch out.

June I didn't know that.

Gerry (*slapping his stomach and thighs*) Stops you putting it on here and here.

June That's certainly well worth knowing. You've been awfully helpful. Thanks.

Gerry My pleasure. Well, your lunch is nearly ready, so I'll be on my way.

June But you haven't had a chance to talk to Brian. Look, stay to lunch, then you two can have a long talk afterwards.

Gerry That's very kind of you—but I couldn't.

June Why not? We want you to, don't we, Brian?

Gerry Well, of course, if Brian really does . . . (*He looks at Brian*)

Brian (*swallowing*) Yes—of course.

Gerry Then I'd be delighted.

June Good. Brian, get Gerry another drink while I go and cut some chives. Do you like chives in your salad?

Gerry Adore it.

June So do we. I grow it in a little herb garden I cultivate. (*Going*) Lunch in about ten minutes.

June exits to the kitchen

Gerry Well?

Brian Well, what?

Gerry (*inclining his head towards the kitchen*) Do you like her better than the other one?

Brian What's that to you?

Gerry Nothing really. But quite a lot to you, I should think, since I paved the way for her. (*He stretches out in a chair*) I must say it all seems to have worked out very nicely for you.

Brian Why have you come back here?

Gerry Curiosity. I was interested to know what happened afterwards.

Brian After what?

Gerry Oh, come off it, Brian!

Brian If you're referring to Sheila's death, I know nothing more about it than the police told me.

Gerry And what did they tell you?

Brian She was found strangled in her car, in a lay-by about five miles from here.

Gerry Oh, dear. And the police have no idea who did it?

Brian They concluded it was some homicidal maniac she stopped to give a lift to.

Gerry (*shaking his head*) Women really ought to be more careful. How soon after was she found?

Brian You must have read it in the papers.

Gerry I didn't look.

Brian Two days after.

Gerry As long as that? Of course it gave the man—whoever it was— plenty of time to get away. They didn't, by any chance, suspect you of complicity?

Brian How could they? I was miles away when it happened.

Gerry Where? (*Smiling*) Not Salisbury, by any chance?

Brian (*lamely*) My car did happen to break down there.

Gerry (*amused*) I thought it might.

Brian It *did* break down!

Gerry I'm sure it did if you say so. And when you came back here next day?

Brian There was nothing to make me think that anything was wrong. Some of Sheila's clothes had gone, but only one suitcase full.

Gerry Didn't the police ask why she was taking her clothes away?

Brian Naturally.

Gerry And you said . . .?

Brian (*getting angry*) I said what was true! (*He hesitates*)

Gerry (*grinning*) That should be interesting. Do tell me.

Brian I said she wanted a shopping spree in London—and to do a few theatres and see some friends. I was going to join her in a day or two.

Gerry Nice touch, that bit about joining her. (*Looking round*) And you got all this without complications?

Brian Why should there have been complications?

Gerry She hadn't talked or written letters?

Brian What about?

Gerry (*admiringly*) You're good, Brian. You're really good. Much better than I thought you'd be. But then you had such a lot to lose if you made one mistake.

Brian I had nothing to do with her death! The police realized that!

Gerry Not even a little death wish?

Brian Why should I have wished her dead?

Gerry Why, indeed? (*He moves to the kitchen door, opens it and looks in*) All right. She's still in the garden. (*He closes the door and returns*) But the thing I can't understand is your lack of curiosity.

Brian What about?

Gerry I do wish you'd stop answering everything with a question. It's most irritating. What happened here, of course. Do you know she might have killed *me*?

Brian Killed *you*?

Gerry I thought you'd find that interesting. Yes, I think she fancied I was a bit of a suspicious character. Anyway, she got hold of your revolver.

Brian She hadn't it when the police found her.

Gerry No .Luckily I spotted it when I was looking for her car keys, and replaced it there. (*He indicates the desk*) She even told me to wait in the car and shut the door on me. Fortunately, as you know, I had a front door key. After that, everything went according to plan. I was just leaving when you rang up.

Brian I called from Salisbury to speak to Sheila.

Gerry (*in a hard voice*) You called from Salisbury according to plan. The phone rang six times, then stopped.

Brian Look, if you're trying to connect me with Sheila's death, I've got an alibi that's unbreakable! And if you try any funny business, I'll tell the police I saw you hanging round here a few days before it happened!

Gerry I wouldn't if I were you. You see—I've still got this. (*He takes out the key*) Your front door key. That would take quite a bit of explaining.

Brian I never gave you that!

Gerry You saw me take it! You *let* me take it! You left the wig and the mackintosh where I told you to! You told me you and Sheila were breaking up, and you listened to me telling you how we could get away with it! And we have! So don't spoil it by playing the innocent and trying to shop me. Because, if you do, I'll pull you in as deep as I am! You've got what you wanted because I helped you to it. Don't be ungrateful.

Brian (*after a moment; shaken*) You swore there wouldn't be any comeback. I asked you what the pay-off was, and you said there wasn't one. You were doing it for the thrill of doing a really perfect murder. You can't deny you said that!

Gerry I don't. That *is* why I did it. But I don't expect to be treated like this when we happen to meet again.

Brian Happen! You came here deliberately.

Gerry True.

Brian *And* you put June up to doing what she did to shake me.

Gerry I didn't see why you should have it all a bed of roses.

Brian I see. Now we're getting to it. What is it you want?

Gerry To stay here.

Brian *Here?*

Gerry Yes.

Brian What the hell for? Are you broke or something? Because if you are, I can . . .

Gerry No, I'm never broke. You should know that.

Brian Then why?

Gerry Because I have a fancy to, that's all. I don't see why we shouldn't get on quite well together. I shan't offer to pay my way. You can afford to keep me for a bit.

Brian Christ!

Gerry Actually, I have another reason as well. You could say I want to stay here for the fun of it.

Brian Fun!

Gerry Oh, not for you. The fun for me. The fun of watching you squirm—keeping you on tenterhooks. The fun of seeing you pouring me a Coke when you'd like to give me arsenic. The fun of hearing you swallowing your words when you'd like to damn me to hell. I think it'll be rather enjoyable.

Brian Look, I'll give you ten thousand pounds . . .

Gerry But I don't want it. I've told you what I want. To stay here for as long as I choose. And you've no choice but to let me.

Brian Why?

Gerry (*producing the key*) Because I hold this key.

They look at each other for a moment. Then June calls from outside the door

June (*off*) Will someone open this door, please? I've got both hands full.

Gerry moves to open the door

Gerry Sorry.

June enters with three dishes

June Thanks.

Gerry Let me take that. (*He relieves her of one dish*)

June Mind, it's hot.

Gerry My hands are tough.

June Sit down. I've only one more thing to bring in.

June goes into the kitchen

Gerry I leave it to you to tell her I'm staying.
June (*calling: off*) Brian, pour the wine, will you?
Brian (*calling back*) All right. (*To Gerry*) Or would you rather have Coke?
Gerry No, I'll try gracious living for a bit. But get in a stock of Coke when you next order.

June enters with the final dish, and an extra set of cutlery

June sits at the dining-table. Brian brings the desk chair, on which Gerry sits

June All right. All set. (*She starts to serve*) When are you going to change that wheel, Brian?
Brian I'll do it after lunch. (*He pours the wine at the bar*)
Gerry I'll give you a hand.
Brian Thanks.
June Then you can give Gerry a lift to wherever he's going. (*To Gerry*) Where are you making for?
Gerry Nowhere in particular. (*He looks at Brian*)
Brian (*swallowing*) As a matter of fact, I thought as Gerry wasn't in a hurry to get anywhere, he might care to stay with us for a day or two. (*He brings the glasses of wine over and sits*)
June (*surprised*) Stay? Yes, of course, why not?
Gerry Oh, but I couldn't.
June Why couldn't you?
Gerry It would be an imposition.
June Oh, nonsense. Brian wouldn't have suggested it if he thought that.
Gerry Would you like me to stay, Brian? Really?
Brian Yes—of course. Be a pleasure.
Gerry Then I will. Thank you. Thank you both very much.
June (*lifting her glass*) Well, cheers.
Brian Cheers.
Gerry (*smiling at Brian*) Happy days.

The Lights fade to a Blackout

SCENE 2

The same. Two weeks later. Evening

Gerry, dressed as before, sits knitting the sleeve of a sweater. A Coke is by him, and he looks the picture of ease and comfort. "The" record is playing softly. Coffee and cups are on the bar. After a moment, June appears on the stairs. She wears an attractive dressing gown.

Gerry (*looking up and smiling*) Feeling better?
June Much. I just lay there and let the dirt of London soak out of me.

Gerry Nothing like a bubble bath, I always say. Coffee's ready. (*He starts to rise*)

June Don't disturb yourself. I'll do it. Do you want some? (*She pours herself a cup*)

Gerry No, thanks. I'll stick to Coke.

June How you can continually drink the stuff . . .!

Gerry It has medicinal properties.

June Rubbish. I'd be running to the loo all day, if I drank as much of it as you do.

Gerry There you are then. You can't say that's not healthy.

June It'd be damned inconvenient in my business. (*She looks at his knitting*) I say, you are getting on with that. (*She sits*)

Gerry Only the rest of this sleeve to do. My going-away present to Brian.

June You won't go till I come back, will you?

Gerry I think I should. Brian may prefer to be on his own.

June I'm sure he wouldn't. He's absolutely helpless without somebody to look after him.

Gerry Well, we'll see what he says.

June (*stretching and yawning*) Ought I to be doing something about supper?

Gerry All under control. I've got the oven on automatic.

June Oh, good.

Gerry What time's your flight tomorrow?

June Not till the afternoon, thank God. Brian's driving me to Gatwick.

Gerry Any packing I can do for you?

June No, it's all done. I don't have to take a great deal, anyway. The film people are providing all my wardrobe. I tried it all on this morning.

Gerry Is it super?

June It's fantastic. If they're selling the clothes afterwards, I shall ask Brian to buy them for me.

Gerry Are you wearing a mink?

June Yes. But not as good a one as Sheila's was. By the by, who came and took all her clothes away? Brian said I could give them to my friends, but when I looked, they were gone.

Gerry They aren't gone.

June But the wardrobe's empty.

Gerry I put them all in my room.

June In your room? Why?

Gerry I knew how much you thought of them, and it seemed such a pity to part with them willy-nilly . . .

June You mean Brian doesn't know?

Gerry No. I thought, after a while, he'd forget what they looked like, then you could wear them if you wanted to.

June I know you meant well, Gerry . . .

Gerry You don't think I should have done it?

June No, I don't really think you should. I know what I said, but they could be a horrible reminder to him . . . Get rid of them while I'm away.

Gerry All right.

June I'll give you some phone numbers, or you can sell them, if you like.
I don't suppose Brian would mind if you kept the money. He said give
them away.

Gerry If I do, I'll give it to you.

June But you may need it.

Gerry (*smiling*) No, I shan't.

June (*after regarding him for a moment*) You *are* odd, you know.

Gerry Do you mean what I think you mean?

June No, I don't. I mean I simply can't make you out.

Gerry What's puzzling you?

June Well, here we are, all living together like life-long friends, and I
don't know a thing about you.

Gerry Does that matter?

June Not really, I suppose. But someone without a background—well,
they're incomplete. They lack a dimension.

Gerry Come to that, I hardly know anything about you.

June There's hardly anything to know. Born in Sudbury, twenty-six years
ago. Drama school—rep-actress—bit player in films, typist and sales-
girl in between. Hoping soon to become Mrs Brian Hamilton. That's me
in a nutshell.

Gerry You're over modest.

June No, I'm not. I'm a realist.

Gerry (*after consideration*) Yes, I believe you are.

June Anyway, that's not my point and you know it. I'm not the odd man
out. *I* didn't knock at the door and say I once met Brian for half an
hour, and then proceed to become one of the family.

Gerry (*with a twinkle*) How did *you* meet Brian?

June You're side-tracking again! (*Amused*) Oh, all right, if you must. I
was on holiday.

Gerry Alone?

June Yes. In my business, your friends are very seldom free at the
same time as you are. The Mini packed up with dirt or something in its
carburettor, and Brian happened to come along.

Gerry Also alone?

June He was in some fabulous car he was testing. Anyhow, he got the
Mini going again, and we arranged to meet that evening.

Gerry Wonderful introducers, cars. Nearly as good as dogs.

June That's how it all began. Now it's your turn. Come on, give! (*Suddenly,
as if she may have been inconsiderate*) Unless, of course, you'd rather
not.

Gerry I don't mind in the least, but you won't find it interesting.

June I'll stop you if I find it boring.

Gerry Could you sling me over the tape-measure? It's by your elbow. (*She
throws it*) We can't have Brian with one sleeve longer than the other.
(*As he measures*) Where do you want me to begin?

June Well, where do you come from originally?

Gerry Exmoor. A council house on the edge of.

June (*laughing*) Liar! With *your* accent.

Gerry There *are* good schools near Exmoor, you know. Haven't you read *Lorna Doone*?

June *You* have, evidently. All right, you were born in Devon, of poor but honest parents.

Gerry Somerset, actually. But I didn't say they were poor or honest.

June Don't say they were crooks!

Gerry No, I think they were like most people. Honest when they had to be, and crooked when they could get away with it.

June What was your father?

The music stops

Gerry He was a clerk in a solicitor's office. He used to cycle there and back twice a day, and on Sundays they'd both cycle morning and evening to the Wesleyan Methodist Chapel. He said it kept him fit. But that didn't prevent him dying at forty-three—or my mother.

June They're both dead—both your parents?

Gerry Yes.

June How?

Gerry A motor coach accident. They'd saved up all the year to go on a tour of Scotland. It happened on the motorway coming home. I was on a camping holiday in Wales, when the police came and told me.

June What a terrible thing. How old were you?

Gerry Seventeen.

June What on earth did you do? Had you finished your schooling?

Gerry Fortunately, yes. I'd already got a job in a hotel—I was hoping to become a chef eventually. It was lucky I'd chosen that, because they let me live in.

June You mean you were left entirely on your own?

Gerry Yes, I hadn't any other relatives. I stayed at the hotel for a couple of years, then I got restless. I decided I wanted to see the world, so I started on my travels. I only came back from Italy at the beginning of this year.

June Haven't you ever thought abou* settling down? You can't go on with this roving life for always.

Gerry Oh, I don't mean to. I think I shall start to think about settling down fairly soon. (*He rises to take her cup*) Fill that up for you?

June Thanks.

Gerry (*as he does so*) Our music's stopped. Shall we have some more?

June (*absently*) If you like.

Gerry (*handing her cup, then going to the record-player*) Why so thoughtful?

June It's curious—what you've told me—so unexpected. It doesn't seem to fit in with you at all.

Gerry Disappointed?

June I wouldn't say disappointed. Just surprised.

"The" record starts again

Oh, not that again!

Gerry Why not?
June You never put on anything else.
Gerry I like it.
June So do I, but there are limits.
Gerry It belongs to one of the pleasantest times of my life.
June What time was that?
Gerry When I first came here. The first time I met Brian.
June (*surprised*) You heard it then?
Gerry Yes.

June looks at him puzzled, a nagging at the back of her mind. Gerry starts folding up his work

What time did Brian say he'd be home?
June He didn't exactly. But I should think about eight. (*Remembering*) Oh, blast!
Gerry What?
June I forgot to put my car away.
Gerry I'll do it in a minute.
June Thanks. Brian hates me to leave it out. He goes on about paintwork and chrome and condensation and what-not, if I do. You can use my Mini while I'm away, if you like. So long as you're not an L driver.
Gerry Oh, no, I passed my test this year. Thanks, it'll be a great help for shopping and so forth. And that reminds me, talking of cars, I always wanted to ask you what became of the Fiat?
June The Fiat? What Fiat?
Gerry (*busy tidying up*) Sheila's car. The one she was driving that night.
June I didn't know what car she drove. How did you know it was a Fiat?
Gerry (*unperturbed*) I suppose Brian mentioned it to me.
June Yes.
Gerry I expect he got rid of it. He'd hardly like to keep it after what happened.
June No.
Gerry Well, I'll put your car away before I forget it. Want to watch and see I don't scrape off any of the paint?
June (*suddenly*) Wait a minute. I forgot, we're nearly out of cigarettes. Would you mind getting me some from the pub?
Gerry There's a box of fifty upstairs.
June Brian will need those, and I shall want some for the morning.
Gerry O.K.

Brian's car is heard arriving and then stopping

Here's the lord and master.
June (*going to her bag*) Get two hundred. Here's the money.
Gerry Right.

Brian opens the front door

Brian You've left the Mini out.

Gerry I'm putting it away as soon as I've got June some cigarettes.

Gerry goes out

In a moment the Mini is heard to start and drive off

Brian You needn't have troubled. I've got plenty, and you can get some on the plane.

June I know. It was only an excuse. I wanted him out of the way for a bit.

Brian Well, I must agree. It's nice to be on our own for a while. (*He kisses her*) Everything go well this morning?

June Yes, fine. There's coffee if you want it.

Brian Thanks. (*He hears the music*) Oh, blast, you've got that ruddy record on again!

June I didn't put it on. It was Gerry. I'll turn it off. (*She does so*)

Brian (*pouring coffee, then sitting*) I wish you'd put it in the bloody dustbin.

June goes to him

You look very seductive. Have you been sitting with Gerry like that?

June I don't think it would matter if I sat with him naked. (*She sits at his feet*)

Brian You smell divine. We'll go to bed early tonight, shall we?

June Ah-ha. (*Smiling*) You've got a long abstinence in front of you.

Brian Six weeks is a hell of a time for you to be away. You promise we'll be married as soon as you get back?

June You fix everything and I'll be back on the first possible plane.

Brian kisses her hair

Brian . . . ?

Brian Yes?

June I've been asking Gerry about himself.

Brian (*alert*) Oh, what sort of things?

June About his background and so on. Has he ever told you anything?

Brian Yes—I think he did a bit when we first met. We chatted for about half an hour.

June Did he tell you anything about his parents, for example?

Brian is silent

Try to remember.

Brian (*uneasy*) His parents—I think he said he had a stepfather. They didn't get on. That's why he left home.

June is silent

Isn't that what he told you?

June No. He told me both his parents were killed in a motor accident.

Brian Well, I could have got it wrong. He wasn't here very long.

June I should think a motoring accident would be something you in particular would remember.

Brian I'm sorry. I don't. Was that all?

June No. Brian—when you brought him here that night—the night you nearly ran him down—the house was empty, wasn't it?

Brian You know it was. I'd been on my own for two weeks.

June Sheila hadn't come back, by any chance?

Brian No. She rang up shortly after I'd got in, and came round about ten minutes later.

June Had Gerry gone by then?

Brian Look, what is all this about?

June No, tell me. Had he gone?

Brian Yes.

June Where?

Brian How the devil should I know? He just pushed off. What does it matter?

June I don't suppose it matters at all. Only one or two things he said seemed very odd to me.

Brian Such as?

June Well, about that record, for instance. I asked him just now why he liked it so much, and he said because he heard it the evening he first came here.

Brian That's rubbish! You know I never play the thing.

June I know. That's why it puzzled me.

Brian I expect you misunderstood him. Come to think of it, I believe he did put it on while I was in the kitchen getting us something to eat. Sheila had probably left it on top of the turn-table, and he just switched it on. That's not very mysterious, surely?

June No—I agree it could have been that . ..

Brian Well, then?

June But there are still one or two other things that puzzle me. You say he was gone when Sheila arrived?

Brian Yes.

June Then how does he know what car she drove?

Brian He doesn't.

June He does. He asked me what you'd done with the Fiat.

Brian Perhaps he'd read it in the newspapers.

June He couldn't have done. If he had, why, when I answered the door to him, should he think I was Sheila?

Brian (*getting in deeper*) Well, I may have mentioned it since. You know I'm always talking cars.

June You haven't! I'm positive. Even I didn't know what make it was.

Brian (*rising abruptly and going to the bar*) What the hell does it matter, anyway? More than likely he was on his way down the drive when Sheila arrived. He's always been crazy about cars since he was a kid. That's why he was so thrilled about my racing trophies.

June Then you'd think he would have learned to drive before this year, wouldn't you?

Brian He's been driving for ages . . . (*Suddenly he realizes he may have been indiscreet*) Is that what he told you?

June Yes, when he offered to put the car away.

Brian Well—I—I may only have assumed he'd been driving longer, because of his interest.

June (*rising*) You didn't, Brian! You *knew*. It was a lie—a deliberate lie. And so was the yarn he spun me about his parents.

Brian (*suddenly afraid*) All right—all right! They were both lies! So what? They were harmless, after all. Some people are compulsive liars—they can't help it. And anyway, why are you behaving like this about him all of a sudden. I thought you liked him.

June I don't like being lied to.

Brian Oh, for God's sake!

June It makes me wonder what else there is we haven't found out. (*She goes to the stairs*)

Brian Where are you going?

June I want to look for something. Put the latch down on the door so he can't walk in on us.

June exits upstairs

Brian, now worried, drops the catch on the front door, then goes to the bar and pours another drink

June returns, carrying a passport

Brian, look at this!

Brian Where'd you get that passport?

June From his hold-all.

Brian But you can't go——

June I'll put it back. I wanted to check if he really had been abroad this year.

Brian Well, had he?

June Yes. But I found something else. Do you know what date he got back to this country?

Brian No.

June (*showing the passport*) He arrived back in England on February nineteenth. Two days before Sheila was murdered.

Brian For crying out loud! So did hundreds of other people, I expect! You're not trying to suggest he——

June I'm not trying to suggest anything. I'm simply starting to wonder if he's quite as ingenuous as he'd like us to believe, that's all. He's lied to both of us—about comparatively unimportant things, I admit. But he also made two admissions—by accident—that make me wonder if he was anywhere around here at the time of Sheila's death.

Brian Oh, rubbish! He was miles away by then.

June How do you know?

Brian He told me he was moving on.

June Exactly. He *told* you.

Brian But if he'd been anywhere around here when she was discovered, he'd have been picked up for questioning—and he wasn't.

June Sheila wasn't found until two days after she was murdered. He could have been miles away by then.

Brian I'm positive he had nothing to do with it. And I'm surprised that you, of all people, should think he might have.

June Why are you defending him so whole-heartedly? When he first came back here you acted as if you couldn't bear him.

Brian I simply thought he had a bit of a nerve—barging in here like he did on half an hour's acquaintance. But anyone can see he's not a murderer.

June I don't know what murderers look like. I suspect they look and behave very much like other people.

Brian You're working yourself up over nothing.

June Are you so sure it's nothing? Look at the facts! He said he heard that record when he first came here—and you never put it on!

Brian I've explained that. I do remember now. He put it on when I was in the kitchen, and I asked him to take it off.

June Yet now he's with us, he persistently puts it on. Is he trying to annoy you deliberately?

Brian Oh, for God's sake! I've had enough of this!

June I believe he knew I wasn't Sheila when I first met him.

Brian Why on earth should you think that?

June Because I think he saw Sheila the night you brought him here.

Brian I've already said he might have seen her arrive.

June I don't mean just a passing glimpse. I think he saw her properly. And I'll tell you why I think so. You remember bringing her suitcase back from the police?

Brian Yes.

June That was the morning he came back here. I'd just opened it when he knocked at the door. Later, he drew my attention to her wig—it was lying on top of her things. He persuaded me to put it on and get her mink coat.

Brian I don't suppose you needed much persuading. You've always hankered after her clothes. Now, I suppose you'll say he knew I was going to get a puncture, and come back in time to see you in them.

June No, of course not. But I do think now there was something calculating—malicious about it—as if he knew you would have hated it.

Brian All it seems to me is, that you're suddenly deliberately maligning someone you've been ecstatic about for the past fortnight. There's not a shred of evidence against him, nor the slightest reason why he should murder someone he never knew.

June But there *was* no reason for her murder, was there? It was established as a completely motiveless crime. Brian, don't you think we ought to go to the police?

Brian No!

June But only to tell them what we've found out. If he's innocent . . .

Brian No, I tell you! The thing's over and done with! All you've said is a lot of speculative rubbish! It's worth nothing at all. I won't have them digging everything up again!

The Mini is heard approaching

He's here. You'd better go and put that passport back.

June At least, don't let him stay here any longer. While I'm away, tell him to go. *Please*, Brian! Say you're closing up the house—anything—only get rid of him.

Brian All right.

The Mini passes the door to the garage. Later the doors close

Now for God's sake, hurry. And put some clothes on while you're upstairs.

June runs upstairs and off. Brian, looking desperately anxious, takes the coffee things to the kitchen

The front door handle turns, but the door does not open. A key is inserted in the lock

Gerry enters carrying a carton of cigarettes. He slings the carton on a chair and goes and pours himself a Coke

Brian enters from the kitchen

Sorry about the door. I must have dropped the catch down as I came in.

Gerry (*smiling*) Don't apologize. I have my key. Been having a nice long chat about me?

Brian What the hell have you been telling June a pack of lies for? She's been asking no end of questions about you.

Gerry Yes, I hoped she might. (*He sits*)

Brian You *hoped*?

Gerry You've got a bright girl there, Brian. I could see she picked up the points about the Fiat and how long I'd been driving, at once.

Brian But she checked with *me*! I told her what I thought was the truth, long before I realized what she was getting at.

Gerry I knew I could rely on you *not* to cover up for me. Good old slow-witted Brian.

Brian You don't seem to understand! She's beginning to think you might have had something to do with Sheila's murder!

Gerry Well, of course. That was the idea.

Brian Are you quite crazy?

Gerry Don't be absurd. You should know I never do anything without a reason. She can suspect as much as she likes, but she won't be able to prove anything.

Brian Then why lead her to suspect anything at all?

Gerry Because I don't want her here any more. I want her to get out.

Brian You *what?*

Gerry You heard me.

Brian And what the hell is what she does to do with you, may I ask?

Gerry Quite a lot. You see, I've come to a conclusion. I've made up my mind to stay here for good, and I don't want her around. You and I will be perfectly happy on our own.

Brian (*after a moment*) You and I? You *are* crazy if you think I'm going to give June up to live with you!

Gerry (*calmly*) I always said, if you remember, I'd find somewhere eventually to settle down. This is it.

Brian All right—I'll give you the damn place. But I'm marrying June and you're not going to stop me!

Gerry (*taking up his knitting*) After June has been in Spain for a week or so, you'll write her a letter saying you want to break it off with her.

Brian I'll be damned if I will!

Gerry You'll say that for some time you've known that marriage with her would be a mistake. Put any reason you like—you don't love her enough, or you don't think she loves you enough—I'll help you write it. The point is, you don't want to see her again. You can offer her money, if you like. You can afford it.

Brian This is what you've been working up to all the time, isn't it?

Gerry No. I've had an idea from the start that this pad might suit me, but I've only just become quite certain.

Brian Have you finished?

Gerry For the moment.

Brian Then you can pack your bloody grip and get out of here right away! I'm not standing for any more of your blackmail! This is the end!

Gerry There won't be any more. This is all I want.

Brian And it's the one bloody thing you're not going to get! You can't implicate me without implicating yourself, and I'm far more in the clear than you are! It's my word against yours, and I can easily tell the police I suspected you of being a shady character when I first brought you in here.

Gerry Did you ever tell them about that first meeting of ours? No, I see you didn't. Don't you think they might wonder why you suppressed such an important piece of evidence for so long? Also, they might wonder why—having entertained such suspicions of me—you then proceeded to harbour me in your house for over a fortnight.

Brian I should say I wanted to watch you—hoped you might give something away.

Gerry (*smiling*) Dear Brian—you and Dr Watson.

Brian All right! They can reprimand me if they like, but I've got a clean record. You've got a history of shady dealings. What about that money-running—that hit-and-run business, and God knows what else? They'll dig them all out! Whereas I've got a fool-proof alibi, and no reason for wishing Sheila dead!

Gerry No?

Brian We were a happily married couple, as far as anybody knew. Nobody knew there was a divorce pending, and nobody thinks it odd if a widower decides to get married again six months after his wife died.

Gerry You're right in the clear, aren't you, Brian?

Brian Yes, I am, so I advise you to get out and stay out!

Gerry (*placidly knitting*) Would you know Sheila's handwriting if you saw it?

Brian Of course I would. Why?

Gerry On the night she came here to collect her things, she left you a letter.

Brian I never found it!

Gerry No, fortunately, I noticed it, and read it.

Brian Where is it? Show it to me.

Gerry Oh, no, I don't think it would be safe with you. But I can show you a copy I had photostated, if you like.

Gerry takes the letter from his pocket and hands it to Brian, who snatches it and reads it

All about regretting the divorce is necessary, and hoping you won't find life too hard without her money. Much better phrased, of course, but that's the gist of it. Quite enough to make the police inquisitive about you, don't you think?

Brian Why didn't you tell me about this before?

Gerry It was my ace in the hole, in case you proved obstinate.

Brian (*beginning to crack*) I never wanted you to kill Sheila! You know I didn't!

Gerry Do we have to lie to each other?

Brian I'm not lying! You did it to satisfy your own murderous instincts! Oh, God, why did I ever have to meet you?

Gerry You'll get over June. Don't forget you were quite ready to give her up once before. And you've got all that lovely money. You can buy yourself a Maserati or a Rolls-Royce Camargue, if you want to. We'll have a yacht at Monte Carlo, a villa in the Seychelles and a flat in Venice. I won't mind you having as many affairs as you like. I'm not a jealous type. You'll find the ephemeral quite as good as the permanent, you will really.

Brian Why did you deliberately make June suspicious of you?

Gerry Ah, now the reason for that was very subtle. You see, I wanted to separate you in as natural a manner as possible. So the best way to do it was for me to become the bone of contention, so to speak. The more she spoke against me, the more you had to defend me. I'm right, aren't I? You've been doing that already this evening while I was away. You're not going to have your best friend maligned by her, so naturally a coolness springs up between you. I'll bet you anything her first letter from Spain will be asking if you've got rid of me yet.

Brian (*after a moment*) I offered you money before . . . If I doubled it . . .?

Gerry Same answer. Nothing doing. (*He puts down the knitting*) I really ought to be seeing about supper. (*Rising*) Open the wine, will you?

Gerry goes into the kitchen

Brian looks at the letter, folds it and puts it in his pocket, then goes to the bar, selects a bottle of wine, and proceeds to uncork it

June appears on the stairs and descends, having changed into a long skirt and frilly blouse

Brian ignores June. She comes up to him and slips an arm through his, lovingly. Brian pulls himself away

Brian Just let me get on with this, will you?

June stares at him. He goes on doggedly with what he is doing, as the Lights fade to a Blackout

SCENE 3

The same. Evening, three weeks later

There are now great banks of flowers in the porch, and vases about. Some cushions have also been changed, indicating a different taste. Brian sits at the desk typing laboriously. Every now and then he stops and takes a drink from the glass of whisky by him. He looks unkempt. He unwinds the sheet of paper from the typewriter and reads it, then, with an exclamation of annoyance, screws it up and throws it away from him. Gerry appears on the stairs. He wears a beautiful velvet suit. He carries a large box

Gerry (*seeing the screw of paper*) That's untidy. Pick it up.

Brian rises, picks up the screw of paper, and flings it into the wastepaper basket. Gerry brings the box to the sofa and sits, taking off the lid. Brian takes his glass to the bar and refills it

You're drinking too much.
Brian What's it to do with you how much I drink?
Gerry Quite a lot. I don't want a travelling companion who's a lush.

Brian in turning, knocks over a vase of flowers on the bar

Look out! There's a duster underneath. Mop up the water before it marks.
Brian (*standing the vase up*) Why the hell do we have to have the house looking like Kew Gardens?
Gerry I like a house to be attractive. Neither you nor your concubine had the slightest idea of gracious living. Did you type your report?
Brian I made a botch of it. It doesn't matter, anyway. It's the last one I shall do.
Gerry How do you know?
Brian Hell's bells, aren't we going away next week to spend all that money you've had your beady eyes on!
Gerry One should never deliberately throw away a means of earning a

living. I'll type it for you later. How do you like these? (*He displays several beach shirts which he has taken from the box*) They have shorts to tone. (*His manner is not in the least effeminate*)

Brian Where are they for?

Gerry South of France—Bermuda—wherever I eventually decide we shall go. You ought to start getting some things.

Brian I can get them where we finally land up.

Gerry I do think you might take some interest in our trip.

Brian Don't push me! For the love of Mike, don't push me! I have to go along with you—do what you want to do, but don't expect enthusiasm on top of it!

Gerry I really can't see why.

Brian If you can't, there's no sense in my talking.

Gerry All right. Are you staying in this evening?

Brian What else is there to do?

Gerry You could go down to the pub for a bit.

Brian No, thanks.

Gerry You must know I don't mind.

Brian I don't care if you bloody well mind or not! I've been there once since June went away, and that was enough.

Gerry Don't your friends wonder what's happened to you?

Brian They know what they *think*'s happened to me! Banks of bloody flowers being delivered to the place—an obvious fairy living here! My friends are *men* and they draw their own conclusions.

Gerry I'm sorry. I never meant my intention to subject you to that as well. Never mind. You'll have every opportunity of demonstrating your manhood when we go abroad.

Gerry rises, putting the box aside

By the way, I had the confirmation of our Sealink booking this morning.

Brian Oh, yes.

Gerry I haven't made any reservations at hotels in France, though. I thought we could stay at any place that took our fancy. Once we're on the Route Nationale there's no knowing how far you may want to drive.

Brian Shall I have any choice?

Gerry Oh, for God's sake, do snap out of it, Brian! You've got away with murder—you're worth a bomb. We're going on a fantastic holiday—we can go round the world if we want to. What have you got to beef about?

Brian *You.*

Gerry (*smiling*) If you get what you want in this world, you generally find it brings its own problems. I may not be the companion you would have chosen——

Brian You can say that again.

Gerry —but you'll find I can be an interesting one. Incidentally, we'd better give Mrs Abbott notice when she comes on Friday.

Brian She gave *me* notice yesterday.

Gerry Oh. Why?

Brian For the same reason that I can't go down to the pub.   .

Gerry Oh, well, we can manage by ourselves for the last few days. Though, it's awkward about the house. I was hoping she'd come in and air it every now and then.

Brian It's curious we haven't heard anything about the London flat by this time. (*He takes a pack of cards from the desk drawer and sits at the coffee table, laying them out for patience*)

Gerry Oh, I forgot. There was a letter for you from the estate agents. (*He takes a letter from his pocket, rises, and gives it to Brian*)

Brian (*taking it*) When did this come?

Gerry This morning.

Brian opens the letter

Is it the cheque?

Brian Yes.

Gerry Good. You can pay it into the bank tomorrow and get our traveller's cheques.

Brian Why didn't you give it to me this morning? I could have done it then.

Gerry I told you. I forgot.

Brian It's a funny thing you always forget to give me my letters till hours afterwards. What others haven't you given me?

Gerry There was nothing else for you today.

Brian I don't mean today! I mean other days! (*Rising*) I believe you've been keeping back some of my mail. For instance, why haven't I heard from June?

Gerry Probably because she hasn't written.

Brian She'd have answered my letter. I know she would! I bet you've kept it back from me, you bastard!

Gerry (*contemptuously*) Control yourself.

Brian Don't sneer at me! (*He seizes Gerry's arm and twists it behind his back*) Answer me, or I'll break your arm!

Gerry (*quietly*) Let go of me.

Brian, after a moment, releases him

There *was* an airmail from June.

Brian When?

Gerry Last week.

Brian Last week!

Gerry I saw little point in letting you have it.

Brian Give it to me!

Gerry All right. (*He takes an opened letter from his pocket and hands it over*)

Brian You've opened it.

Gerry I thought it best.

Brian moves away with the letter. Gerry sits and takes over the patience

Brian She doesn't believe the reason I gave for breaking it off.

Gerry Of course not. No woman ever believes a man can fall out of love with her. It's a wound to her vanity.

Brian She thinks it's your influence.

Gerry Naturally. She has to blame someone. Oh look, two queens, one after the other.

Brian sits, staring at the letter

You may as well destroy that. You won't be answering it. And any other letter that may come you'll disregard. Just as you'll disregard any attempt she may make to see you.

Brian You bastard! You bloody bastard! (*He drops the letter on the sofa table*)

Gerry Don't be melodramatic. She never meant that much to you. You're not sorry about her—you're just sorry for yourself. It's your subjection to me you can't take, that's all.

Brian You've destroyed me! You've utterly destroyed me!

Gerry If you'd only face up to it you'd find that practically nothing has changed. I have to dictate to you a bit while we're still here because you're so incautious. Once we're abroad, you can be as free as air. Look, I'll be even more generous to you.

Brian Generous!

Gerry Much as I like this house, I won't even insist we return to it when we come back. We'll sell it and find somewhere else to live, so you can make a new start in a new neighbourhood. I can't be fairer than that.

Brian You'll always be there.

Gerry That is the understanding.

Brian Why do you want to be? How can you bear always to be with someone who loathes you?

Gerry stops with the cards and looks at Brian contemplatively

Gerry You're just like my step-father. He's the same blustering, sporty type; heavy drinker; thinks himself a dog with women. More than anything in the world I'd like to have stepped on his face.

Brian So instead, you're stepping on mine. You've got a hate complex about him, and I'm the scapegoat.

Gerry I never understand about complexes. All I know is, I've got what I wanted. And—apart from one very small item, soon to be replaced—so have you. (*Looking down at the patience*) It's come out. Do you want the cards?

Brian No.

Gerry (*rising*) I'll put them away, then. (*He puts them back in the drawer*) I'm going upstairs to sort out the clothes I shall be taking with me. Then I thought we might eat at *Le Petit Français*. That suit you?

Brian Yes.

Gerry Good. Saves me cooking.

Gerry picks up the box and is going to the stairs when the telephone rings. Gerry goes to get it, but Brian is first

Brian Hello . . . hello! . . . Push in the coin! Hallo . . . (*He replaces the phone*) Some idiot in a call-box.
Gerry Probably a wrong number. Ring up the *Français* and make a reservation, will you?

Gerry goes upstairs and off

Brian takes off the receiver and dials

Brian Hullo . . . Good evening. I'd like to book a table for two tonight . . . About half past eight? . . . Hamilton . . . Thank you. (*He hangs up, and moves towards the bar. Then he remembers June's letter. He picks it up, looks at it, then tears it across and drops it into the wastepaper basket. He takes the revolver from its drawer and looks at it, then in despair he puts it back. He goes to the bar and pours himself a drink. Moving in his aimless way towards a chair he stops, thinking. He puts down his glass, goes to the wastepaper basket, and takes out the pieces of June's letter. He brings them down, lays them on the table and finds the piece which has her address and telephone number. He claws up the rest, throws them away again, then moves to the telephone. He looks towards the stairs, then lifts the receiver carefully and dials "100". He waits impatiently. After a moment he speaks quietly*) This is Dorking seven-oh-nine-six-two-one-five. I want to put through a call to Barcelona . . . Yes, of course, Spain . . . What? I can dial it direct? Well, can you tell me how? . . . Look this is terribly urgent. Can't you do it for me? . . . Oh, all right. Just a moment. (*He finds a pad and pencil*) Yes? (*He repeats after the operator*) oh-one-oh—three-four—three (*He writes*) Then the number. Thank you.

Gerry appears on the stairs. He is dressed in the blonde wig and mink fur coat that Sheila wore. As before, he looks beautiful and astonishingly like her. He comes quietly downstairs and sits in an armchair watching Brian

Brian replaces the receiver, lifts it again, and dials the first six digits. Then he moves the scrap of paper towards him

Gerry I wouldn't do that if I were you, dear.

Brian gasps and swings round, staring at him

Put it back, there's a good boy. You're not to be trusted an inch, are you, love?

Brian drops the phone and covers his face, moving to a chair. Gerry rises and replaces the phone on its cradle

Brian Take those things off! You know I can't bear to look at you like that!
Gerry I know, darling. That's why I thought you needed a little lesson. Every now and then you forget what you've done, don't you?

Brian I did nothing! You know I did nothing! I'd have stopped you if I'd thought you really meant it. I swear I would!

Gerry (*kneeling by Brian*) Look at me, Brian—look at me!

Brian turns his head slowly

This is exactly how Sheila looked. The way she did her hair—the coat she wore the night she was murdered. Poor rich Sheila, the girl you once loved—slept with—swore to love and cherish. Don't you think its only right you should pay a little for breaking all those promises?

Brian You swore you'd got rid of those things!

Gerry I shall never get rid of them. Every now and then we shall have this little masquerade, until you've finally made up your mind you've no alternative but to settle down with me.

Brian I think you want to drive me mad!

Gerry (*insinuatingly*) Shall we go abroad as husband and wife, Brian? You still have a double passport, haven't you? What fun it would be. I bet nobody would ever suspect.

Brian rises convulsively, and goes to the desk. He takes out the revolver and levels it at Gerry

Brian Look, I know you think me a fool—I know you think you've got me cornered . . .

Gerry I *know* I have.

Brian All right, you have. I admit it. I know I've got to play along with you if I want to keep my freedom. But I have got a breaking point, and you're bringing me closer and closer to it! Lay off me, will you! Stop goading me! Don't ever try that dressing-up trick with me again—or I swear by everything that's holy, I'll kill you!

Gerry Did you know the chances of a revolver shot being fatal are about forty to one?

Brian I've got six shots in here. That should reduce the odds.

Gerry I don't think we'd better go out to dinner tonight. You're obviously not in the mood. There's cold meat and salad in the fridge. We'll make do with that.

Brian (*still covering him*) So long as I'm understood.

Gerry Loud and clear.

Brian All right. Get changed while I forage for us. (*He puts the revolver in his pocket, and goes towards the kitchen*)

Gerry I'll phone the restaurant.

Brian Remember, I meant what I said.

Brian goes into the kitchen

Gerry looks after him for a moment, then moves to the telephone and dials

Gerry Good evening. I believe Mr Hamilton made a reservation for tonight . . . Yes, for two. Would you mind cancelling that, please? . . . Thank you. I'm so sorry. (*He replaces the receiver and pulls off the wig*)

Gerry goes upstairs and off

For a moment the room is empty, then a key is heard softly in the front door lock—the door is opened cautiously

June enters. She is dressed in a trouser suit, and her hair is concealed under a head-scarf. She looks at the banks of flowers in the hall, and the changes in the room, in surprise   ·

Brian enters carrying some cutlery and a cloth. He stops as he sees June

Brian June! (*Coldly*) How did you get here?

June (*in the same manner*) I used my key. Do you want it back?

Brian No, I mean—I thought the film—is it finished already?

June No, but I have a few days off. I flew back from Spain this morning.

Brian (*laying the cloth*) What for?

June In view of your warm welcome, it now seems rather stupid, but I wanted to see you.

Brian Oh. I didn't hear your taxi.

June I left it at the bottom of the drive. I didn't want to advertize my arrival if there was anybody else in the house. That's also the reason why I hung up when you answered the phone just now.

Brian The phone? Was that you in the call-box?

June Yes. Look, you needn't be afraid I've come in hopes of persuading you to marry me. In fact, I'm not at all sure I would marry you now. I only want to know, for your own sake, what's going on.

Brian (*laying cutlery*) Nothing's going on.

June Oh, Brian!

Brian After you'd gone away, I—I thought things over, and—well—I felt we'd made a mistake, that's all. I'm sorry if I hurt you . . .

June Of course you hurt me. But if I believed that was your true reason for breaking it off I'd never have come here. But I know perfectly well it isn't. Your precious little pal made you do it!

Brian Why on earth should he?

June That's exactly what I want to know. Why? Brian, I'm not an idiot, and I'm not blind! That day he came back I could see you hated him—more than that—you were afraid of him!

Brian That's rubbish!

June Then why haven't you got rid of him? I begged you to before I went away. Yet he's still here. The very look of this room tells me that.

Brian I wanted him to stay. I asked him to.

June Even after I told you how he lied to me?

Brian I explained that.

June You didn't. All you said was some people are compulsive liars. Some people are compulsive murderers, too, I suspect.

Brian (*terrified*) Be quiet! He'll hear you!

June Where is he?

Brian Upstairs. June, for God's sake, go away and leave me alone!
Things have got to be like this. There's no help for it.

June Why have they got to be like this?

Brian They have to be, that's all.

June Has he got some sort of hold over you?

Brian No.

June Please—if he has, won't you tell me? I'm not asking anything for
myself. I'll go out of your life if you want me to. Only, if there's something wrong and I'm sure there is—let me try and help you.

June touches Brian. He breaks away

Is it something to do with Sheila's death? Is he trying to implicate you
in some way?

Brian (*at the end of his tether*) Shut up! Shut up! I can't take any more!
For Christ's sake, go away and leave me alone!

*Brian sits, his fists pressed against his forehead. June looks at him for a long
moment, then glances towards the stairs. She looks back at Brian*

June (*quietly*) Did he kill Sheila?

Brian, his face still hidden, inclines his head

Then why are you protecting him?

Brian (*looking up*) It started the night I first brought him here. I thought
he was gone when Sheila came, but he was somewhere listening. You
didn't know this, but she was going to change her will—cut me out of
everything. When she'd gone he came back, and told me how he could
kill her. He'd killed before and got away with it. He was sure he could
get away with it again. He called it the Murder Game.

June What did *you* have to do?

Brian Nothing—only be well out of the way when it happened. I said he
was a maniac and told him to get out. When I heard of Sheila's death
I was as shocked as you were.

June Why didn't you tell the police all this? Were you afraid to?

Brian Yes.

June But you had your alibi.

Brian He knew what my alibi was. It was all part of his plan.

June You knew exactly when it was going to happen?

Brian Yes.

June The night you were at Salisbury?

Brian Yes. I didn't really believe he'd do it, but I daren't take a chance.

June You could have warned Sheila.

Brian I told you! I didn't really believe he'd do it!

June But you took care of your own skin. And this—your living together—
is the price of murder?

Brian No. He swore there'd be no come-back—that he was doing it for
kicks. When he turned up again, you know I was going to get rid of
him. Then he showed me a letter Sheila had left that night—he took it,

of course. It said about how we were breaking up, and that I'd get no money. It was the perfect weapon against me.

June Why did I have to be got rid of?

Brian He had a fancy for us to live together. I offered him money, but he wouldn't take it. This was what he wanted. I'm sorry, June—I'm sorry.

There is a pause. Then June moves to the bar and pours him a drink, bringing it to him. While he is gulping it, she goes to the telephone pad, and writes on it quickly. She tears off the page and brings it to Brian

What's this?

June (*whispering*) Read it. I can't say it. He may be listening.

Brian (*staring at the paper*) For God's sake—why'd you do this!

June Give it to me. (*She tears the paper to shreds and drops it in the waste-paper basket*)

Brian I've got to get away!

June (*holding him*) No, Brian, don't run! They'll catch up with you in the end. Stay and face it! You didn't kill her!

Brian You stupid bitch! Do you think I want to spend the rest of my life in prison! (*He thrusts her aside and runs upstairs*)

June No, Brian, please stay! I'll wait with you!

Brian exits upstairs

June looks after him hopelessly

Gerry enters from the kitchen. He has changed back into his own clothes. He carries a suitcase, and the mink coat is over his arm

Gerry You'll never persuade Brian to go to the police, you know. All you've managed to do is persuade him to pack a case and do a bunk down the back stairs. Fortunately, he won't manage to get away. I've disabled both the cars. (*He locks the kitchen door*)

June Have you been listening?

Gerry Most of the time. Then I went to fetch this for you. (*He indicates the case*) I'm sure you'd like to take the rest of your things away now.

June Aren't you afraid?

Gerry Afraid?

June Now I know you murdered Sheila?

Gerry Not in the least. Candidly, I should have thought the boot was on the other foot. (*He moves to the bar*) May I offer you something?

June No.

Gerry (*opening himself a Coke*) Your film must have ended sooner than you expected.

June I have to go back to Spain the day after tomorrow.

Gerry But you took time off to try and rescue Brian from little me. You didn't quite expect what you got, did you?

June I didn't know you turned him into a murderer as well.

Gerry Oh, Brian's not really a murderer. Though mind you, he could be a potential killer if he were driven into a corner. (*He takes a sip of his drink*) Do sit down.

June No, thank you.

Gerry Did they turn you into a blonde for your film, by the way?

June Yes.

Gerry Do show me.

June I'd rather not.

Gerry Why? I'm sure it suits you.

With a swift movement he comes to her and pulls off her scarf, throwing it on to a chair. Her long fair hair cascades down. He stands back admiringly

Oh, beautiful. I knew you'd look gorgeous.

June makes a move for the scarf

No, don't cover it up. Did they give you a mink, too?

June Yes.

Gerry But not for keeps, of course?

June No.

Gerry Never mind. I've kept you Sheila's.

June I don't want it; thank you. I shouldn't like the way I got it.

Gerry I do think scruples are so idiotic. Well, it's there if you change your mind. (*He moves to the bar and holds out a dish*) Salted peanut?

June shakes her head

Well, now you know I murdered Sheila, don't you want to know how it was done?

June I know how it was done.

Gerry Oh, you mean the police idea about thumbing a lift from her? That was just nonsense. It all took place in this room.

June In this room?

Gerry Yes. I'll show you how, shall I? You be Sheila and I'll be me.

June No!

Gerry But its quite fascinating. The beauty of it was its sheer simplicity. Everything was rather like it is now, except that the room was darker—(*he moves and draws the curtains*)—and only this lamp was on. (*He switches on the lamp*) Oh, yes, and her particular record was playing. (*He switches on the player*)

June *That* was when you first heard it!

Gerry (*smiling at her*) Clever girl. A coat was on this chair—(*he puts the mink coat on the chair*)—and her wig. (*He throws June's scarf on the chair*) That will do for the wig—and her suitcase was over here. (*He puts the suitcase by the porch*) Well, that's the set-up. Then I knocked at the door.

June Did she let you in?

Gerry Oh, yes, just as you did, if you remember. We chatted a bit, then I persuaded her to give me a lift in her car.

Outside an engine turns over furiously but does not start

That's only Brian trying to start the car. Take no notice. (*He picks up the coat*) Then she put on her coat. (*He holds it for June*) Come on, you're Sheila.

June reluctantly slips into the coat

Then I noticed her wig. (*He holds out the scarf*) She went to put it in her suitcase—well, go on. Put it in.

June, after a look at him, moves to the suitcase and bends to open it. Gerry takes a length of thin cord from his pocket and moves softly behind her

That was when I killed her.

He goes to slip the cord over her head. June turns in time

June No!

June struggles and manages to fling Gerry off. He pursues her to the stairs

The front door is flung open and Brian enters in a fury, the revolver in his hand

June pushes Gerry off and runs towards the kitchen

Brian What have you done to my car! (*He sees June's back as she runs across the room, and thinks it is Gerry still in disguise*) I warned you, you bastard!

Brian fires. June screams and clutches her arm, staggering

Gerry (*from the shadows*) Good old Brian! You can save me the trouble!

Brian stares at him in horror, then looks at June

Brian (*moving to her*) June! I didn't know . . .

June pushes past him and makes a staggering run to the front door

Gerry (*screaming*) Stop her, man! Finish it! (*He rushes at Brian to get the gun*)

June exits through the front door

At the same moment a police siren is heard faintly. Gerry and Brian stand and listen

It's coming here!
Brian She told the police.

Gerry stares at Brian, then runs to the door

Stand still! (*He levels the gun*)
Gerry I can fix the car! With your driving they'll never catch you! Let me go and fix it!
Brian You're not going anywhere.

Gerry Don't be a fool! You'll get years if they get you!

Brian (*steadily*) Whatever stretch I get, you'll get double. I'll have the satisfaction of hearing you squeal. I'll step on your face, you bastard!

The police siren is much nearer

Gerry For God's sake . . . (*He moves to Brian*)

Brian (*gripping him*) You always wanted us to be together. Well, this time —so do I.

The police car pulls up outside, as—

the CURTAIN *falls*

FURNITURE AND PROPERTY LIST

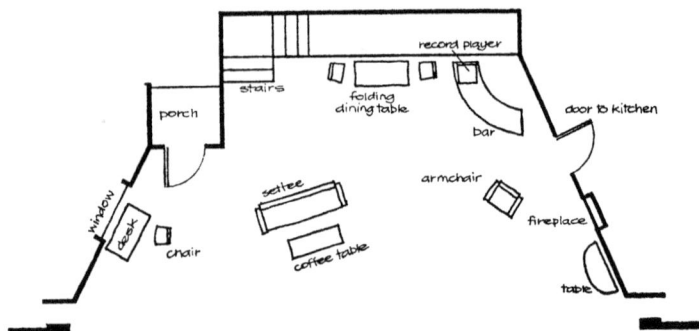

ACT I

On stage: Settee. *On it:* cushions
Armchair
3 small chairs—two at dining-table, one at desk
2 bar stools
Record-player and records on bar
Dining-table. *On it:* vase of flowers
Desk. *On it:* photo of Brian, lamp, telephone, directory, pad and pencil. *In pigeon-hole:* revolver. *In drawer:* door key, photo of Sheila, pack of cards. *Beside it:* wastepaper bin
Coffee-table. *On it:* ashtray
Bar. *On it:* ashtray. *On shelves under and behind it:* tins of Coca-cola, bottles of whisky, sherry, wine, various drinks, soda syphon, water jug, glasses, corkscrew, bottle-openers
On shelves in recess: silver trophies
In porch: potted plants
In fireplace: small electric fire
Carpet
Stair carpet
Window curtains

IN FIRST BLACKOUT
Strike: Hold-all (removed by **Gerry**)
Set: Curtains open

IN SECOND BLACKOUT
Set: Wig and mackintosh on chair
    Hold-all as before

IN THIRD BLACKOUT
Strike: Empty glasses and Coke tins
Set: Check wig and mackintosh as before
    Curtains open
Off stage: Hold-all, with envelope containing wads of notes **(Gerry)**
    Tray with 2 plates, knives, plate of bread, cheese **(Brian)**
    Sheila's white mackintosh **(Gerry)**
    Wig **(Gerry)**
    Suitcase **(Sheila)**
Personal: **Brian:** door key, watch, car keys
    Sheila: handbag, with door key, car keys, letter
    Gerry: coin, handkerchief, dark gloves, passport

ACT II
SCENE 1

Strike: Any dirty glasses, Coke cans

Set: Typewriter, typing-paper, carbon paper, on desk
    Typed envelope on desk

Off stage: Tablecloth **(June)**
    2 knives, 2 spoons, 2 forks **(June)**
    Travel brochures **(Brian)**
    Sheila's suitcase containing wig and white mackintosh **(Brian)**
    Apron **(Gerry)**
    Mink coat **(June)**
    3 plates and cloth **(June)**
    Serving-dish of food, server, 1 knife, fork, spoon **(June)**

SCENE 2

Strike: Any dirty glasses, Coke cans
    All dishes, plates, cutlery, etc.

Set: Small chair in original position
    Wool, knitting-needles, half-finished sweater, Coke can, glass, on
      table for **Gerry**
    Tray with 3 coffee cups and saucers, coffee-pot, milk, sugar, spoons,
      on bar
    Tape measure by **June's** chair

June's handbag, containing money, on bar
Bottle of wine on bar shelf
Curtains closed

Off stage: Gerry's passport **(June)**
Carton of cigarettes **(Gerry)**
Photostat letter **(Gerry)**

SCENE 3

Strike: Knitting, tape-measure
Coke can and glass
June's handbag
Cigarette carton
Bottle of wine

Set: Banks of flowers in porch and in vases on furniture, including bar
Typewriter, typing-paper, carbon paper, glass of whisky, on desk
New settee cushions
Curtains open
Check revolver in desk pigeon-hole

Off stage: Large box containing beach shirts **(Gerry)**
Letter and cheque in envelope **(Gerry)**
Airmail letter, opened **(Gerry)**
Sheila's wig and mink coat **(Gerry)**
Cutlery and cloth **(Brian)**
Suitcase **(Gerry)**

Personal: June: door key

Suggested record: "I Get A Kick Out of You"

LIGHTING PLOT

Property fittings required: wall brackets, outside porch light, table lamp, electric
    fire
Interior. A sitting-room. The same scene throughout

ACT I. Evening

To open: Room in darkness

Cue 1	**Brian** switches on lights *Snap on wall brackets*	(Page 1)
Cue 2	**Brian** switches on porch light *Snap on outside porch light*	(Page 1)
Cue 3	**Brian** switches off porch light *Snap off outside porch light*	(Page 1)
Cue 4	**Brian** switches on fire *Electric fire up*	(Page 11)
Cue 5	**Brian** switches off lights *Blackout except for fire*	(Page 15)
Cue 6	**Brian** switches on desk lamp *Snap on lamp and covering spots*	(Page 15)
Cue 7	**Gerry**: "... this is what would happen...." *Fade to Blackout*	(Page 17)
Cue 8	When ready *Fade up to brackets on, lamp off, fire off*	(Page 17)
Cue 9	**Gerry** switches off lights *Blackout except for dim exterior lighting*	(Page 19)
Cue 10	**Gerry** switches on brackets *Return to previous lighting*	(Page 19)
Cue 11	**Gerry** switches off lights *Blackout except for dim exterior lighting*	(Page 19)
Cue 12	After car drives off *Fade to Blackout*	(Page 19)
Cue 13	When ready *Return to Cue 6 lighting*	(Page 19)
Cue 14	**Brian** looks in drawer *Fade to Blackout*	(Page 22)
Cue 15	When ready *Fade up to brackets on, lamp and fire out*	(Page 22)
Cue 16	**Gerry** switches off lights *Snap off all interior lighting*	(Page 25)

Cue 17	**Gerry** switches on lights	(Page 25)
	Return to Cue 15	
Cue 18	**Gerry** switches off lights	(Page 25)
	Return to Cue 16	
Cue 19	After car drives away	(Page 25)
	Fade to Blackout	

ACT II, SCENE 1. Morning

To open: General effect of daylight

| Cue 20 | **Gerry:** "Happy days." | (Page 38) |
| | *Fade to Blackout* | |

ACT II, SCENE 2. Evening

To open: Brackets and table lamp on

| Cue 21 | **Brian:** ". . . get on with this, will you?" | (Page 50) |
| | *Fade to Blackout* | |

ACT II, SCENE 3. Evening

To open: Effect of fading daylight. Interior lighting off

Cue 22	**Gerry** draws curtains	(Page 59)
	Dim all lighting	
Cue 23	**Gerry** turns on lamp	(Page 59)
	Snap on table lamp and covering spots	

EFFECTS PLOT

ACT I

ACT II
Scene 1

Cue 17	**June** exits after laying cutlery *Car approaches and pulls up*	(Page 26)
Cue 18	After **Brian** exits *Car starts up and drives away*	(Page 28)
Cue 19	**Gerry** starts record-player *"The" record plays*	(Page 32)
Cue 20	**Gerry** exits to kitchen *Clatter of saucepans*	(Page 32)
Cue 21	**Brian** switches off record-player *Music off*	(Page 33)

Scene 2

Cue 22	At start of Scene *Music from "The" record*	(Page 38)
Cue 23	**June:** "What was your father?" (approximate cue) *Record reaches end and stops*	(Page 41)
Cue 24	**Gerry** starts record-player *"The" record plays*	(Page 41)
Cue 25	**Gerry:** "O.K." *Car arrives and stops*	(Page 42)
Cue 26	After **Gerry** exits *Sound of Mini car starting up and driving off*	(Page 43)
Cue 27	**Brian:** ". . . digging everything up again!" *Mini car approaches*	(Page 47)
Cue 28	**Brian:** "All right." *Mini passes front door—car doors close*	(Page 47)

Scene 3

Cue 29	**Gerry** goes to stairs *Telephone rings*	(Page 53)
Cue 30	**Gerry** switches on record-player *"The" record plays*	(Page 59)
Cue 31	**Gerry:** ". . . a lift in her car." *Car engine turns over furiously, but does not start*	(Page 59)
Cue 32	**June** exits *Police siren, starting faintly then growing louder*	(Page 60)
Cue 33	**Brian:** ". . . so do I." *Police car draws up outside front door*	(Page 61)